Praise for

CHASED by an ELEPHANT

"In a time when God's standard for sexual morality is increasingly washed away by a flood of enticing, distorted material targeting vulnerable young people, this is more than an important book for parents, teens, and church leaders, it is a MUST READ. Using marvelous metaphors and written with compelling clarity, *Chased by an Elephant* is a clarion call to every adult responsible for guiding children and youth through today's licentious culture. Graham explores these critical issues of our time with clarity, intelligence and always from the perspective of gospel principles and the light of truth."

—Kieth Merrill, Academy Award winning filmmaker, writer and director of *Legacy* and *The Testaments*.

"There is no other book as engaging on sexual manners as this one. *Chased by an Elephant* opens dialogue on an often hushed area so parents and young people are free to talk about thoughts, feelings, and actions from a moral and spiritual perspective. The clarity on gender maturity, importance of distinct gender roles, and why chastity retention is so important are well explained. A strong sense of masculinity for boys and a strong sense of femininity for girls are presented throughout—a crucial foundation for the prevention of homosexuality. This book takes all we know about healthy gender and sexuality development and presents this information in a way that is least offensive and easily grasped. I recommend that parents get their hands on this book!"

—Dawn Stefanowicz, Author, *Out From Under: The Impact of Homosexual Parenting*

"Parents need this book. Their children need this information. We live in a time when sexual propaganda is directed at children, adolescents, and young people and is increasingly infiltrating our education systems. Traditional values and religious freedom are continually disparaged and threatened by the secular, sexual movement through political and legislative channels. While public opinion is conditioned into mindless and arbitrary political correctness and error, LDS families have the opportunity to stand strong and immovable on the Lord's side. Here is a thoughtful, conversational book illuminated by the gospel of Jesus Christ which educates and empowers parents. It prompts them to fulfill their parental obligation to discuss sensitive, relevant, and crucial topics with their precious children and guide them along the right path."

—Gayle Ruzicka, President, Utah Eagle Forum

"I congratulate the author on covering one of the most emotional draws Satan uses to keep people from knowing the truth. A person's dominating emotion determines what he will do at any given moment, and Satan uses sexual lusts to keep God's children in spiritual darkness. The best way to overcome Satan's program is for each family to help each child understand the Lord's program and all the ways Satan will use to get them off track. This book covers the facets of both programs and encourages parents to cover each topic with each child at the appropriate time according to levels of maturity. It will help parents know what must be discussed in order to prepare each child to handle the gravitational pull of Satan's program."

—James B. Cox, Author,
How to Qualify for the Celestial Kingdom Today

"This book by Janice Graham is worth a careful read, particularly by parents. It is a thought-provoking and alarming commentary on what is happening in our sex-saturated culture. Of particular concern is the damage that can come from premature labeling of children and adolescents. Such labeling sexualizes children and places them at risk for a variety of problems. The book deserves careful attention and has the potential to make an elephant-sized difference."

—A. Dean Byrd, PhD, MBA, MPH

"Janice Graham deserves praise for authoring Chased by an Elephant. In a straightforward and light-hearted way, Mrs. Graham successfully guides parents in imparting the virtue of chastity to their children in the context of the Latter-day Saint tradition."

"Teen sex is NOT values neutral. Teen pregnancy, STIs and emotional heartache due to extra-marital sexual activity do not strike those who embrace chastity: the life-long virtue that places human sexuality at the service of love. Parents should also heed Mrs. Graham's advice to affirm their children's inherent dignity as male or female. That there are inherent gender differences is a truism fast disappearing from our culture much to the detriment of our children's mental and physical health."

—Michelle A. Cretella, MD
Chair of the Committee on Adolescent Sexuality,
American College of Pediatricians

CHASED by an ELEPHANT

CHASED by an ELEPHANT

The Gospel Truth about
Today's Stampeding Sexuality

Janice Barrett Graham

Published by:
Tidal Wave Books
www.tidalwavebooks.com

Produced by:
The Standard of Liberty Foundation
www.standardofliberty.org

Book design by Camille G. Turpin

Cover art by Andrew S. Graham and Lili Ribeira.
Cover design by Lili Ribeira.
Inside illustrations by Andrew S. Graham and Lili Ribeira.

Printed in the United States of America

First printing May 2010.
Second printing Aug 2010.

Library of Congress Cataloging-in-Publication Data available

ISBN 978-0-9724770-5-5

To the young,
who, as all wise men since Plato have observed,
have to be taught
what they should respect as valuable and beneficial
and what they should reject as worthless and detrimental.

The author acknowledges the helpful suggestions
and encouragement received from expert professionals
in the preparation of this book. It is the author's hope
and prayer that those in positions of authority and influence,
such as therapists, scientists, professors, ecclesiastical leaders,
and publishers, produce a great stack of much better books than
this one on these subjects, with only God and the worth of souls
in mind and regardless of the opinion of the world.

Table of Contents

Introduction for Parents

The misconduct many LDS parents fear most while raising their children is sexual immorality. Young people acting out sexually results in tragic consequences. Besides the lost innocence, emotional problems, and physical health risks associated with these bad choices, church-related expectations compound the problem. Due to unchastity, families must deal with the shame and crisis of church discipline, an unwanted pregnancy, a postponed or canceled mission or temple marriage, or a turning away from the Church.

The number of our young people involved in sexual sins has greatly increased in recent years. Some of the most stalwart-seeming youth find themselves involved in pornography, premarital sex, promiscuity, homosexuality, and the like. This trend is not surprising when you consider that American culture has become increasingly secular, sexually permissive, and technological. All manner of propaganda is pervasive in mainstream forums, including our education systems from kindergarten through college. Combined, these conditions are unprecedented. Children of all ages are being bombarded with falsehoods about inherent male and female roles, sex and sexuality, love, marriage, procreation, religion, and history. This harmful exposure is evident in the lives of many young people through a variety of psychological problems including anxiety, depression, gender confusion, addictions, and even suicidality. And sad to say, this exposure is practically inevitable. As one author put it, "I guarantee you that there are Amish kids in Pennsylvania who ride in buggies and don't use zippers who know who Madonna is!" Referring to the easy accessibility of pornography to children, a TV commentator proclaimed, "Evil is in the house."

Many parents are doing all they can to protect their children from such harm, but they should know that even the best safeguards have loopholes. This book is for those parents who may be asking themselves what more they can do to prevent tragedy or help correct the course of a wayward child.

Parents may not realize that attitudes about sex, sexuality, marriage, and procreation do not come naturally, but are taught. With the cultural acceptance and promotion of radical feminism, abortion, pornography, premarital sex, and homosexual relationships, think about what is now being taught to young impressionable minds on a grand scale. Today's parents must purposefully teach the truth about these issues or their children will learn false and dangerous ideas from the world around them.

Even more important, parents must internalize and apply, and teach their children to internalize and apply, the basic principles of the gospel of Jesus Christ. Because youth are being lured and ensnared by sexual sins like never before, parents are presented with an outstanding opportunity to handle these problems the Lord's way. Elder Boyd K. Packer testified, "I have long believed that the study of the doctrines of the gospel will improve behavior quicker than talking about behavior will improve behavior." Alma knew that the word of God was more powerful than anything else in leading the people to do that which was right (Alma 31:5). If parents are really concerned about preventing or helping their child recover from sexual sin, the gospel of Jesus Christ is not only the best way, it's the only exalting way.

Sooner or later children are faced with some aspect of the world as it is. They will make their own choices, a process that will involve some degree of error. In the spiritual sense, whether these sins are small or large doesn't matter. If otherwise well-brought-up children are given no understanding of human nature and the need for divine redemption, we are putting them in a vulnerable and dangerous position. For example, if they are outwardly obedient but have not been taught to seek and recognize the influence of the Holy Ghost, we may find them slipping into sexual sin. If they lack the spiritual tools to recover and learn from their errors, we may find them despairing, rebellious, defensive, unteachable, past feeling, or turning to self-destructive escapes and addictions.

While it is proper to do all we can to protect children from bad influences, encourage their participation in Church and other wholesome activities, and teach them traditional values, as Latter-day Saints we must encompass these activities and teachings within the gospel of Jesus Christ. More than anything else, today's youth need a knowledge and conviction of the characteristics of each member of the Godhead: of Heavenly Father's loving plan toward perfection, of Christ's essential and redemptive Atonement, and of the whisperings of the Holy Ghost which will teach them all they must know, do, and become.

This book combines the parental responsibility for teaching children both the basic principles of the gospel and the proper attitudes toward human sexuality. It illuminates how to apply gospel principles to everyday blessings and obligations, including those associated with God-given gender and developing sexual feelings. The practical and gospel information outlined here is indispensable to your child's spiritual growth as well as physical well-being.

Even very young children can be taught to apply basic gospel principles. Children of all ages can begin now to practice gospel applications in every situation. Knowledge and daily application will prepare them to recognize God's unchanging truth about their sexuality when the time comes. Children are being exposed to dangerous material and false ideas about sex and sexuality at increasingly earlier ages, and will need to be taught correctly at increasingly earlier ages. They must be continually provided with the truth in order to counteract what the world is teaching. A strong spiritual foundation is essential.

This book is written for parents to use with their growing children. Parents should become familiar with the concepts in this book from beginning to end before presenting it to their children. The text is worded as if the author is addressing children around age 10 and up, but parents should judge at what ages to present the material according to the needs and maturity of each of their own children.

The twelve short chapters may be read aloud as a family or to individual children. The material may be taught in casual discussions such as at mealtimes or on walks, rides, or outings. The book may be utilized in planned settings such as regular Family Home Evening lessons or father and child interviews. Parents may invite some children to read the chapters on their own.

This book can help open communication on sensitive issues, encompassed within gospel truths, that are best presented and discussed within the home. It can help create a safe and matter-of-fact environment where children feel free to ask questions and confide concerns of a sexual nature. It is hoped that parents will talk with their children about the concepts introduced throughout the book as moved upon by the Spirit. For example, in chapter six, you may be reading aloud to children, "As young people grow up, it is likely that they'll experience [sexual feelings] to some degree and feel curious. They may want to ask questions and learn about them from a trusted source." At this point you may feel prompted to stop reading and say something like, "If you have any questions about sexual feelings, we can answer them. We hope you feel comfortable asking us." Whether or not the child has experienced sexual stirrings, it might be a good time to explain that those feelings are a normal part of your child's development in preparation for marriage and family.

In the interest of readability, we have avoided interrupting the text with footnotes. Several pages of supporting references and resources, including many quotes from LDS General Authorities, appear at the end of the book for further study.

The material in this book can motivate and assist parents in their sacred obligation to continually and thoughtfully exemplify and instill in their children the principles of the gospel of Jesus Christ and the truth as it relates to today's stampeding sexuality. Boyd K. Packer said, "[F]ailing to teach and to warn and to discipline is to destroy. . . . We did not make the rules; they were revealed as commandments. . . . In spite of criticism or opposition, we must teach and we must warn." Armed with knowledge, humility, and faith in the Lord, young people have a much better chance of avoiding serious sins and tragic consequences, or quickly returning to the right path.

1
What Elephant?

– the meaning and purpose of chastity –

We believe in being honest, true, chased by an elephant, virtuous, and in doing good to all men . . . just kidding! That's just what some Primary kids came up with when they didn't understand the words *chaste* and *benevolent.* Of course there's no elephant in the 13th Article of Faith. But if you aren't quite sure what the word chaste means, an elephant might help.

Take the African Bush Elephant. It's the biggest land mammal there is, twice as tall as a man and weighing up to eight tons. That's sixteen thousand pounds, the weight of a semi truck. And yet these huge animals can be trained by human beings who are quite small by comparison. People ride elephants and teach them tricks. They also train them to lift and haul lumber and do many other useful tasks. Even though elephants are big enough to crush people, they can be taught to control their strength and obey commands.

How can a man train an elephant many times his size? The easiest time to train an elephant is when it's a baby. But even a baby elephant is large, so the trainer must first use strong restraints to keep the baby elephant in control. The animal can then

To be chaste means to keep our sexuality inside a certain boundary.

be taught to follow certain directions, step by step. Soon the baby elephant gives up trying to wander off and is restrained with only a small rope. When the elephant is full grown it remembers the rules it learned when it was young and stays put even though it could easily break free.

Just like the elephant learns to stay within a certain boundary set by his trainer, we can learn to be chaste, that is, keep our sexual thoughts, feelings, desires, and behaviors within the boundary set by Heavenly Father. Chastity is also called sexual purity or sexual morality.

Sexual feelings are part of Heavenly Father's plan for His children. As we grow into adulthood, our physical development naturally includes sexual development. Healthy and proper sexuality encourages us to marry. It enables a husband and wife to have a natural family of their own. The process of bringing Heavenly Father's spirit children to earth is called procreation. Sexual desire and procreation are profoundly connected. They form a power that is one of many gifts from Heavenly Father.

Sexuality presents choices. Heavenly Father wants us to use this desire only for what it is intended, so He gave us the law of chastity. He makes sure that this law is well known to His children through scriptures, prophets, and the light of Christ. This law is the boundary for sexual feelings, thoughts, and conduct. But God also gives us the gift of agency. We can choose to obey or disobey the law of chastity. One way we show our love for Heavenly Father is by keeping the law of chastity.

What exactly is the law of chastity? It is quite simple. *The Family: A Proclamation to the World* introduces it nicely. It says,

"The sacred powers of procreation are to be employed only between man and woman, lawfully wedded as husband and wife." We can also find it referred to in the *For the Strength of Youth* pamphlet. "God has commanded that sexual intimacy be reserved for marriage [between a man and a woman]." Outside of marriage we must strive to restrain our sexual thoughts, words, feelings, and conduct. In marriage, sexual thoughts, words, feelings, and conduct are lovingly and wholesomely focused on our husband or wife. Anything else is unchaste.

You might wonder why we need boundaries. Here we can get some more help from the elephant. Did you know that elephants don't jump? If they did, their tremendous weight would crush the bones of their own feet. Jumping is definitely out for elephants, but they do have a way of running that looks like fast walking. An elephant that gets riled up can really move. Once a circus elephant that suddenly went crazy was recorded on camera. The animal began to run in what looked like slow motion. Its long legs took gigantic steps. Its big ears flapped angrily. Its massive head and trunk swung violently. It smashed down fences and gates. It demolished cars. All anyone could do was scramble to get out of the way until weapons were brought in to put the unfortunate elephant down.

> **The law of chastity is well-known and quite simple.**

Elephants are one of Heavenly Father's creations. They are good and fascinating creatures. But elephants are so big and strong that they can be extremely dangerous. That's why they must be trained carefully if they are going to be around people.

Like the African Bush Elephant, human sexuality is good and fascinating too. But this power can be very dangerous unless there are boundaries or rules. Obeying the law of chastity prevents us from committing sexual sins and getting ourselves in serious trouble. Without the law of chastity someone is bound to get hurt.

Some of the hurtful consequences associated with sexual sins affect people inside their minds and hearts. They fail to value themselves as sons and daughters of Heavenly Parents. They don't relate appropriately to others. They forget what their purpose is in coming to the earth. They don't care about what Heavenly Father wants for them. They don't want to think about Jesus and his Atonement. They lose the companionship of the Holy Ghost.

Other hurtful consequences of sexual sins occur on the outside and affect others. Babies are conceived and born to unmarried parents into an unstable and inadequate environment. Some mothers tragically choose to destroy their babies before they can be born. (This is called abortion and is legal in all fifty of the United States, with some restrictions such as how late in the pregnancy they can be legally performed and by whom.) Church membership and temple blessings are disrupted or lost. Missions are postponed or canceled. Marriages end and homes are broken. Sexually transmitted diseases (STDs) are spread, some of which take away the ability to bear children. Some STDs are incurable, and result in suffering, misery, and even early death.

> **Without chastity, someone is bound to get hurt.**

Sinful sexual behaviors that cause these tragedies are nothing new. Other names for these behaviors are sexual immorality, sexual impurity, licentiousness, and unchastity. There have always been people who choose to step outside God's law of chastity and act badly. But in the past, most everybody looked down on wrong sexual conduct. Civilized societies have always had fairly strict customs and rules for sexual morality so as to keep order and prosper. Now, in recent decades, unchastity has become more acceptable. Rules are being broken without any thought of the consequences. Sounds pretty uncivilized, doesn't it?

> **Today unchastity is popular.**

Our modern culture often sends the false message that the law of chastity unduly restricts personal freedom and is old-fashioned. As a result, many people have decided they don't want to obey the law of chastity. They ignore well-established boundaries. A lot of these people are public figures like national leaders, writers, educators, movie stars, and pop singers. Their unchaste ideas and behaviors have spread and become popular.

Along with a rejection of God's law of chastity has come the technology explosion. Nothing like it has happened in the history of the world. As you know, technology has both good and bad sides. One bad side is how through movies, television shows, the internet, and cell phones, many more people are tempted to break the law the chastity. Wrong ideas and temptations about sexuality are all around. Much of today's world is an overgrown jungle of bad information. But in spite of the confusing jungle around you, your sexuality, like the elephant, can be trained to stay inside the boundary God has set in His law of chastity.

> **We're living in a jungle of bad information.**

This law is simple, but in today's world it is often ignored and even ridiculed. The sad consequences of out-of-bounds sexual behavior are not usually mentioned or shown. People tend to deny or cover up the very real causes and problems associated with sexual sins. More than ever, young people need to know what it means to be chaste inside and out. They need to understand why God has commanded them to be chaste. They can be chaste for the right and best reasons, reasons that make sense.

We began this chapter with the 13th Article of Faith. We'll end it with the 1st Article of Faith. "We believe in God, the Eternal Father, and in His Son Jesus Christ, and in the Holy Ghost." To best understand the *why* of chastity we all first need to understand and apply a few basic truths about the Godhead. Here are three important gospel truths you need to know:

The 1st Article of Faith is first for a reason.

1. You need to know that Heavenly Father lives and that He loves you. You are literally His spirit son or daughter. He wants to give you eternal life, the greatest of all His gifts.

2. You need to know that Jesus is your Savior and you need him. Because we are all human and make mistakes as we learn and grow, Jesus Christ, who atoned for our sins and was resurrected, is the only way back to Heavenly Father. When we truly make the Lord the center of our lives, we qualify for God's presence.

3. You need the Holy Ghost, or the Spirit of the Lord, to teach and guide you. Remember, when

> you were born you lost your memory of your premortal life. The gift of the Holy Ghost can witness to you of the truth of all things. It can help you know what's right and what's wrong and keep you moving in the right direction.

Of course Satan wants to stop God's children from returning home. One way he does this is by tempting us with out-of-bounds sexual thoughts and feelings. If he can get us to disobey the law of chastity, he knows we are on one of many tangled jungle paths that lead to forgetting Heavenly Father, Jesus, and the Holy Ghost.

So, why train that elephant? Why be chaste? The best reason is because you love Heavenly Father. We are commanded to love God with all our hearts (Matthew 22:37-38). You can show Heavenly Father you love Him by your desire to obey the law of chastity. This is the kind of unselfishness Jesus showed. He put Heavenly Father first. With this motivation, not only will you be more likely to avoid all those sad consequences of sexual sin, you'll also be growing more like Jesus. The Lord is your best trainer. His voice, which comes to you through the Holy Ghost, is there in part to help you keep your developing sexuality inside the boundaries.

You don't have to be chased by an elephant.

If you obey because you love Heavenly Father, rely on Jesus as your Savior, and seek the Holy Ghost, you will want to keep the law of chastity. You'll be in control of your body rather than your body controlling you. You won't be chased by an elephant, even in this modern-day jungle of bad information.

2

Me Tarzan, You Jane

– the reality of male and female –

Here's a very short quiz. What do these three statements have in common?

1. We see the sun rise in the east.
2. Light travels faster than sound.
3. Human beings are either male or female.

If you think all three statements are *true,* you are right. Every morning the earth rotates to receive the sun's light in the eastern sky. We see a flash of lightning before we hear the cracking, rumbling noise it makes. Parents always want to know if their new baby is a boy or a girl. The three statements above are absolutely true. These truths are based on reality.

Our modern-day jungle spreads the lie that there are no absolute truths. But we know better. Many things are absolutely true. Some absolutes are very important to our health and well-being. Many are even a matter of life and death. How about how the earth revolves on its axis and rotates around the sun? If its

Absolute truths exist.

position and movement were any different, the earth could not sustain life. How about how our bodies need oxygen, food, and water to live? Without these necessities, each microscopic human single cell could not survive. Whether we're talking about something as huge as the solar system or something as tiny as a cell, there are many life-and-death absolutes.

Today, one of those important absolutes—number three above—is being challenged. People are saying that the two sexes are not different or important, even that they do not matter at all. People are insisting that children do not need both a mother and a father. Some are even claiming that two men or two women can be married to each other. Here are some examples. In California a law was passed in 2007 that declares the words *mother* and *father* obsolete in school texts and activities. In a Florida elementary school adults are allowing a boy to act as if he is a girl; he uses a girl's name and wears girls' clothing. Some think their male or femaleness depends on how they "feel," deciding they are male one day and female the next. Others even try to change their gender from male to female or female to male by having doctors tamper with their healthy bodies.

Male and female? Absolutely.

Of course none of the above are right or good. It all sounds more like a science fiction movie than real life. Of course we know the reality of the two sexes. Even Tarzan figured it out pretty quick when he met Jane. "Me Tarzan. You Jane," he said. But today's world has become terribly jumbled up. Denying the reality of male and female is causing a lot of damage and confusion.

You might wonder, why would anyone make such things up? And why would anyone believe them? There are several possible answers to these questions. Here are some:

People make up lies to get something they want. Lies can feel more comfortable or appear more attractive than truth. People often believe what they want to believe, regardless of the truth. When lies get repeated enough times large numbers of people start to believe them. Sometimes people just aren't paying enough attention, or they want to be accepted and liked, so they get drawn into the flow of lies. And finally, lies might contain some truth that makes them easier to believe, and many people don't take the time to think the lie all the way through.

Some people make up and believe lies.

It's pretty tricky, isn't it? The best lies are introduced very gradually and have a little truth, or what appears to be reasonableness, mixed in. It's like how mothers used to give their children vitamins. Years ago, vitamin pills were so bulky, bad-tasting, and hard to swallow, mothers crushed and mixed them with a little honey or jam in a big spoon in order to get their children to take them. Likewise, a tinge of truth can make a lie sound good enough for people to swallow. In this way, lies and misconceptions concerning the two human sexes have been slipped in and are now being acted on as truth in more ways than we can count.

One of the most subtle and slippery ways lies get accepted is through language. Words and phrases have been adopted and given all-new meanings. Words and phrases have even been invented. Of course changes in language and the way we use and define words are nothing new. What's new is that language development has taken an evil turn. Some of the words and phrases that have been adopted, twisted, or invented and which are now being used to confuse the truth about the two

Language can be used to confuse truth.

sexes and God's law of chastity are: freedom, equality, diversity, tolerance, human rights, homosexual, gay, lesbian, bisexual, transgender, sexual orientation, discrimination, homophobic, bigoted, and dozens of others, some of which are extremely vulgar. It is up to us to seek the Spirit to correctly discern the true meaning of words along with the false and inaccurate meanings being substituted.

The two sexes are different for some very important reasons. The most obvious reason is so two people of the opposite sex can get married, have children, and raise a family as Heavenly Father planned. Of course the two sexes are similar in some ways that are not so important. Both men and women can swing from jungle vines, change a tire, do the dishes, and be good doctors and teachers. But they are not the same in ways that are really important. Only the male can fertilize a female's egg. Only the female can conceive and grow a baby in her womb. And after the birth of a baby the father and mother each contribute to raising the child in unique and important ways.

The two sexes are different in fundamental ways.

Did you ever wonder where these absolutes come from? They come from God and have always existed. Truth is not something we can invent as we go along. Truth is not something we find inside ourselves. Truth is discovered. The law of gravity is a good example of a truth being discovered. It was in 1687 that a scientist named Isaac Newton discovered there was such a force as gravity. Now, say Tarzan came from the jungle to the city and decided he wasn't going to believe there was such a thing as gravity. He could even go around saying and doing all kinds of clever, Spiderman-like acrobatics that may convince others that gravity does not exist. But if he tried to jump off a building without his handy vines to swing on, he and whoever was watching would be reminded in a tragic and dramatic way that gravity is real. Splat! When we deny reality there are serious consequences.

Truth is always there.

It's too bad that the absolute truth about male and female is being watered down, tangled up, and even buried alive. But just because some people are on the wrong path doesn't mean we have to be. Many opinions are not based on the truth. Bad ideas and falsehoods should be rejected. You can live your life in harmony with the truth that there are two, and only two, sexes—male and female—with important natural differences.

The Lord has given us many sources of truth to rely on. Let's list some and the truths they reveal about male and female.

Scriptures. Genesis, the first book in the Bible says, "So God created man in his own image, in the image of God created he him; male and female created he them (Genesis 1:27)." Nowhere does the Bible say that God created only man, only woman, or any other type of human being besides male and female, or that male and female are interchangeable.

Prophets. *The Family: A Proclamation to the World* states, "All human beings—male and female—are created in the image of God." This inspired document from the prophet and apostles says that we are spirit sons (males) and spirit daughters (females) of Heavenly Parents. It tells us that being male or female is "an essential characteristic." This was true before we came to earth, it is true while we are here, and it will be true forever. From this we know that whether a person is born male or female is an eternal attribute and should be highly respected.

Scientific Facts. There is no doubt about a person's sex (unless that person is born with a rare birth defect). At birth, whether a baby is male or female is plain to see. Today, parents can even know the sex of their baby by ultrasound long before the baby is born. But physical anatomy is not the only way we know a person is male or female. Every person's sex is also encoded in his or her genes. From DNA scientists can even tell whether a 3,500-year-old Egyptian mummy is male or female!

There are many reliable sources of truth.

History. The world's oldest writings show a great and unmistakable respect for the distinct differences between male and female. The ancient Romans used two different symbols. The symbol for male was the shield and spear of the mythical god Mars: ♂. And the symbol for female was the hand mirror and comb of the goddess Venus: ♀. The ancient Chinese used the words yin and yang for opposites, including male and female. Human history overflows with references to the two opposite sexes. Societies have always encouraged these natural differences in order to survive and prosper. Encouraging the differences between male and female has been essential for the continuation of humankind.

Good Books, Music, Movies, and Art. The libraries of the world are crammed with the truth about male and female. Myths, folk tales, poems, plays, stories, and books are based on the fact that human beings are permanently either male or female. Classic literature shows how this reality greatly affects people's choices and lives. Countless works of music do the same. Operas, symphonies, ballets, musicals, and songs reflect the male/female reality. Museums are adorned with beautiful artworks collected through the centuries, such as sculptures and paintings, that would not exist except for the absolute truth of male and female. And don't forget all the great movies that have been made over the last century that revolve around the inherent differences between men and women. We can think of these resources as wonderful gifts from Heavenly Father that confirm eternal truths.

The Holy Ghost. We talk a lot about the iron rod in Lehi's dream (1 Nephi 8, 11). We say the iron rod is a symbol for the word of God, which we take to mean the scriptures. But the iron rod represents more than a book made of paper and ink. It represents the word of God revealed by the power of the Holy Ghost to each of us. The scriptures become truly valuable when we personally understand them and apply them to our individual lives. The Holy Ghost can make this happen. You must hold fast to the Holy Ghost, as if you are holding to an iron rod, to teach you how to apply the word of God and guide you along the right path (Moroni 10:5).

The Holy Ghost will let you know the truth of all things.

No matter where we get our information about important things, we should check with the Spirit to see if it's true. You can do this simply by praying about it. That way, you have done your spiritual homework, you have drawn closer to the Lord, and you can enjoy your own testimony of whatever truth concerns you. We call this personal revelation. The Holy

Ghost, or Spirit of the Lord, can help you make good choices, help you learn from your mistakes, and should be your number one source of truth.

In this jungle where we live the Holy Ghost is like a spiritual Tarzan. He's always there when you need him to confirm absolute truth and rescue you from dangerous and false ideas. Through the Spirit, you can know without a doubt that every child of God comes in one of two distinct sexes, male or female.

3

Mirror, Mirror on a Tree

– masculinity, femininity, and natural gender roles –

What if you lived outdoors in a real jungle and wanted to see how you appeared to others? You might look at your reflection in a pond. Maybe you'd have a little mirror hanging on a tree. What could you see about yourself? What do other people see when they look at you? How do you present yourself? Does your reflection have anything to do with being either a boy or a girl? Well, it should.

We've talked about the reality of male and female. Now, an important question: Is the right way to act as a boy or a girl something you naturally know how to do perfectly? Or is it something you have to learn? If you think it's something you learn, you are right. Especially today, when some people claim that there are a variety of genders, maleness and femaleness need to be modeled and encouraged to develop properly.

What do you see reflected in the mirror?

When we're babies it doesn't matter too much whether we're male or female. All babies' basic needs are about the same. But parents know their baby's sex is going to matter a great deal

later on. Ideally, parents naturally help their children develop proper gender identification by grooming and dressing them in ways particular to their sex, as is customary. Early on, some say as young as age two, a child actually begins to identify mostly with his or her own sex. In healthy families, little boys naturally imitate their dads. They are developing what we call masculinity. In healthy families, little girls naturally imitate their moms. They are developing femininity. As children grow up, whether they were born male or female gets more and more important. This is in preparation for adulthood, marriage, and family.

Masculine means acting like a male in ways that matter.

By masculine we mean acting like a boy, and then a man, in the ways that really matter. By feminine we mean acting like a girl, and then a woman, in the ways that really matter. For instance, it doesn't seem to matter whether you are a boy or girl when it comes to wearing jeans and liking music and sports. But it does matter whether you are a boy or girl when it comes to growing up, sexuality, marriage, and family. Can you imagine what would have happened if Adam hadn't learned how to be a man and Eve hadn't learned how to be a woman in the ways that matter? No human race!

Up until recently, people have supported the differing male and female roles. It was obvious to everyone that God made women to be wives and mothers and men to be husbands and fathers. In fact, the family is like a miniature society with its own little government. It has opposite-sex parents who unite to organize a family. It can also have male

Feminine means acting like a female in ways that matter.

Men acting like men and women acting like women works best.

and female children of different ages and needs. It has wise grandfathers and grandmothers who encourage the young family and may need help themselves when they are older. A family takes care of its members and protects them from harm. It all comes from males acting like males and females acting like females, just as God intended. This arrangement has always worked best.

But you remember our modern-day jungle of bad information. Some people are now ignoring how men and women have different traits and roles. They push the idea that males should be more like females and females should be more like males. They say that the roles of husband and wife, father and mother, are outdated and unnecessary, even bad in some cases. Girls and boys are often thrown together as if they are just the same. This trend goes against nature. It makes for confusion and disorder when it comes to young people's developing sexuality. The law of chastity is overlooked.

Remember, gender (maleness or femaleness) is an eternal principle. It is important in many ways, even if we don't have the opportunity to be husbands, wives, or parents during this earth life. It is too bad that our culture is reflecting more and more confusion about gender roles. Because of this trend, many people are failing to fulfill their potential as male and female children of God. It puts health and safety, law and order, marriage and family, even freedom, at risk. It blocks people's progress, temporally and spiritually.

Even so, it shouldn't be hard to clear up the confusion. We just have to go back to the important differences between the two sexes. You may wonder how masculine boys have to be. You may wonder how feminine girls have to be. You may ask, how do boys and girls develop the boyish or girlish qualities that matter? These are real concerns in today's world. Following are some things you should know.

Belonging to the Club

Every boy needs to know that he belongs to the Male Club of the World, no membership card necessary. Every male is a full member of this club no matter how he looks or behaves. And no girls are allowed.

Boys and girls are members of their own exclusive clubs.

Every girl must realize that she belongs to the Female Club of the World, no dues required. Every female is automatically admitted no matter what she looks or acts like. And no boys can ever get in.

Of course these clubs are not officially formed, but they exist in a very real sense. Each of us can be sure we are a member in good standing of one of these two clubs: the one that fits our physical body. These two clubs are big and totally exclusive. As much as we need, admire, and love certain members of the opposite sex, they can never belong to our club, and we can never belong to theirs. Some people today are deciding they don't belong to their own club, but this is not true. Some are saying they can switch clubs, but this is not possible.

We are now confronted with alternative sexualized groups which, unlike the obvious Male or Female Clubs of the World, really are officially organized. They give themselves labels such as gay, lesbian, bisexual, or transgender. This is tragic. Anything other than male and female is no group at all. It is an unhealthy denial of the reality that can be seen in a simple mirror. Everyone belongs to their own unique club, Male or Female, no matter what. Permanent membership in your own club is exciting and necessary.

For Tarzans Only

Every boy should feel comfortable with himself as the male person God made him, in his spirit and in his body. It helps to identify with other males. Boys need plenty of activities that do not include girls. They need to interact with other males without competition and distraction from females. They need plenty of opportunities to develop their masculinity. At the same time, they need to accept each other as fellow members of the Male Club of the World.

You should feel accepted in your own club.

Today, some people insist that it's perfectly fine to encourage boys to be more like girls. Examples are how boys are wearing earrings or allowing girls to treat them like one of their girlfriends. This won't do. Some things should be reserved just for girls. Imagine Jane painting Tarzan's toenails while she chats about clothes and other boys! Poor Tarzan.

It is healthy and right for boys to want to be accepted and liked by other boys, to want to be together, to admire, and to love each other. Healthy nonsexual affection between males is important. Unfortunately, there are some boys who miss out on this healthy affection. They have trouble fitting in properly with other boys and men. This can cause problems with healthy sexual development. Boys who have any questions about feeling like they belong to their own club could use some assistance. It's best if they can comfortably go to their parents. Otherwise, they must search out someone trustworthy for facts and reassurance. They should focus on the realities in this book. Most of all, they should apply the 1st Article of Faith. For starters, they could pray about how Heavenly Father lives and loves them. He loves every one of His sons more than we can imagine.

For Janes Only

Every girl should feel comfortable as the female person God made her, in her spirit and in her body. It helps to identify with other females. Young girls need all-girl interactions just as young boys need all-boy interactions. They need places and activities they can call their own without competition and distraction from boys. They need plenty of opportunities to learn to be feminine. They also need to accept one another as equal members of the Female Club of the World.

Today there is a lot of emphasis on girls doing whatever boys do. Examples are how girls are playing on boys' sports teams and joining the military as combat soldiers. Generally, these are not good ideas. Some activities are not appropriate for females. Imagine big strong Tarzan insisting that Jane do all the building of tree houses and protecting from man-eating lions! Poor Jane.

For a number of reasons, some girls have trouble properly fitting in and identifying with other girls and women. This can cause problems with healthy sexual development. Girls who have any questions about feeling like a member of their own club could use some assistance. It's best if they can comfortably go to their parents. Otherwise, they must search out someone trustworthy for facts and reassurance. They should focus on the realities we've talked about. Most of all, they should apply the

1st Article of Faith. For starters, they could pray about how Heavenly Father lives and loves them. He loves every one of His daughters more than we can imagine.

Monkey See, Monkey Do

Monkeys are good mimics. They copy what they see. This is obviously not always a good plan. You wouldn't want to copy someone who was doing something wrong. But it can be a good plan when someone is doing something right, such as demonstrating proper masculinity or femininity. Boys who want to develop more masculine traits, and girls who want to develop more feminine traits, can pick out good examples to follow. They should choose individuals who are humble, modest, confident, and matter-of-fact about their male or female identity. Older siblings, parents, aunts or uncles, grandparents, coaches, teachers, or church leaders might be good choices. Boys and girls can take note of how these people dress, walk, stand, sit, talk, and interact with others. They can consciously try to mirror their masculinity or femininity.

Choose good masculine or feminine role models.

Be careful not to use for your role model anyone who exaggerates their gender identity. In their best form, mannerisms that are truly masculine or feminine are subtle and refined, not pretended or extreme.

Defending the Male Territory

It might be a good idea if, as a sort of exercise, every boy could put on a gorilla suit and pound his chest as a symbol of his maleness. Unfortunately, like a gorilla beats his chest in defense of his territory, real masculinity has to be protected and defended in our modern-day mixed-up jungle.

Boys, stick up for yourselves.

It's a shame when any boy is teased about his biological sex. How confusing it would be to belong to a club, and yet be treated as if you didn't belong and weren't welcome! It can be a hard enough job developing masculinity without your peers pointing out your differences and calling you names. A boy who is teased may begin to feel he isn't the right kind of boy, or that he isn't a real boy at all. This can be very hurtful and even contribute to an elephant stampede later on.

Remember, all boys are boys in the important ways. Usually boys who look down on other boys do so because they are insecure about their own masculinity or membership in the Male Club.

It just so happens that the unfortunate boys who get teased nowadays are usually those who are more talkative, artistic, musical, or studious. Actually, these traits don't have anything to do with real masculinity. Most of the world's greatest talkers, artists, musicians, and scientists happen to be men! If a boy is getting teased or put down about his maleness for these reasons, or any other reason, this is another time when it's important for him to talk to someone trustworthy, preferably his parents. If he doesn't talk to someone who can reassure him, he might start to believe the lies he is hearing from the name callers. He might begin to give importance and false value to the thoughts and feelings he experiences. Boys can become confused about their male identity. If so, they may shy away from their manly responsibilities such as providing for a wife and children or even search out somewhere else to belong. (The same sort of thing can also happen with girls.)

What About Sissies and Tomboys?

When a boy or girl has serious trouble feeling like they belong to their own club, it is called gender confusion. This can be a big problem and require some professional help. But there are less serious problems having to do with gender identity, too, that we simply grow out of. When they are young, some boys and girls don't yet know how to act according to less important cultural rules. They perhaps learn more slowly in this particular area. In the process, for a while they might act as if they aren't sure about their gender. Boys might have girlish interests and girls might have boyish interests, and this doesn't necessarily mean anything. When children grow up generally healthy and happy they eventually put away childish things. If children are shown the proper examples, are accepted in their club, and are given the right information, they mature properly and things come right in the important ways.

There are only two real clubs when it comes to sexuality: male and female. Any other group is pretend.

Others Belong, Too

It's our job to matter-of-factly accept people as Heavenly Father created them—male or female—regardless of their appearance, mannerisms, or interests. But the times in which we live call for more than that. We need to reach out to those who are at risk. We need to support those who struggle to feel confident with their God-given body. We need to encourage those who feel like they aren't full members of their club. For example, at a Young Men basketball activity, a boy with less athletic ability than others should be invited to play. Whether he chooses to play or not, he should be given some manly pats on the back just like all the other boys, rather than be ostracized or teased. Boys should confirm each other's inherent maleness. After all, they are all members of the same club. By the same token, a girl who appears or seems different, such as overly tall or shy, should be treated kindly and included equally with the other girls in their circle of femininity. Girls can help each other by confirming each other's femaleness.

You know the old saying, "Sticks and stones may break my bones but names will never hurt me." Well, names can too hurt, especially when we're young. Be very careful not to use slang words, labels, or names that discount or confuse anyone's gender. Such treatment can cause people to doubt themselves and leave emotional scars that lead to wrong ideas and conduct. It shouldn't be hard to treat everyone with common courtesy and respect. Heavenly Father loves all His children and means for them to fulfill their gender roles in all the important ways.

Boys and girls should take a good look at themselves in a nice big mirror and make sure they are developing subtle traits in harmony with the way God made them, male or female. They can make sure the way they present themselves—their hair, clothes, speech, and conduct—modestly reflects their gender. They can do this because of the love they feel for Heavenly Father and their faith in His plan for them. They can pray often about who they are: a spirit son or daughter of Heavenly Parents. They can pray about how God created them, male or female, and talk to Him about what that means now and in the future. They can talk to Heavenly Father about how much He loves them and how He wants them to mature in every way. They can pray about what

False sexual labels cause damage.

Make sure you're developing proper traits.

He wants them to do and become. For boys, this includes becoming a man, husband, and father in time. For girls, this includes becoming a woman, wife, and mother someday. The Spirit will guide you to represent yourself as the male or female you are in the ways that really matter.

Why is all this so important? Being a strong member of your own club is essential to fully developing your masculine or feminine abilities so you can get along well with the *opposite sex.* A boy has to be confident in his masculinity to fulfill his potential as a son of God and in preparation for marriage and fatherhood. A girl has to feel safe and valued in her femininity to fulfill her potential as a daughter of God and in preparation for marriage and motherhood.

You need to relate well to your own sex before relating well to the opposite sex.

Take a look. Seeing yourself in that mirror as either masculine or feminine is essential to Heavenly Father's great plan for you now and later.

4

Were You Raised In a Jungle?

– discerning good and evil in today's world –

There is an old saying that goes, "Were you raised in a barn?" It might be used at the dinner table to mean something like, "Look out, you're forgetting your manners." Picture how cows casually eat their food off the ground, horses noisily chew with their mouths open, and pigs root greedily in a trough of slops. These are acceptable mealtime manners for animals, but not for humans.

Chastity could be described as sexual manners. Rather than a barn where the animals are tame, our wild jungle comparison comes to mind. When people forget their sexual manners we might wonder, "Were you raised in a jungle?"

Chastity=good sexual manners.

Did you know that some people are using the animal kingdom to justify their bad sexual behavior? They say that if animals do it, people can and should do it, too. It's as if how animals act is the new standard for how people should act! The truth is, animals routinely do all kinds of things no civilized, educated, decent, healthy human being would do.

You are growing up in an unruly jungle where some people act like unthinking wild animals. But of course you have the power, or agency, to choose for yourself to behave properly. You might be wondering where rules for right and wrong conduct actually came from. These rules are not just made up by somebody. Traditional, time-tested rules for human conduct are based on a standard of goodness outside ourselves.

Rules of right and wrong come from outside ourselves.

In chapter two we talked about truth being eternal. It's the same for the important rules for good behavior. Important rules are discovered or revealed. Everyone has access to them through the light of Christ. As far back as we have written records, human beings have operated according to this light, whether they knew it or not and no matter what they called it. You can think of it as goodness, rightness, order, morality, or traditional values. A really simple example of this timeless standard of goodness outside ourselves is how we all know it's wrong to trip an innocent stranger as he walks by. Other examples are how we know it's wrong to lie, steal, or be unfaithful to one's husband or wife.

There are lots of rules like this that men have always recognized. The ancient Chinese called the rules the Tao, or The Good Way. Early Hindus called it the Rta. Ancient Egyptians, Greeks, Romans, Norwegians, and Anglo-Saxons had similar sets of rules. The ancient Jews had the Ten Commandments. When Christ came to earth he approved and added to this same basic standard of behavior to include being good not only outwardly but in our hearts and minds for all the right reasons. What we call Judeo/Christian values

God is the source of goodness.

today embrace these age-old rules. As Latter-day Saints, along with other Christians we know the source for these rules to be God who created us.

Nowadays we hear people say they have found a new, more enlightened set of sexual manners or rules. But they are fooling themselves. (Remember, truth is absolute, not what just anyone wants it to be.) This movement gathered speed in the early 20th century and shot forward in the 1960s. The motto in the '60s among rebellious young people was, *if it feels good, do it*, and it has carried over into today's world. This idea was, and is, and always has been, a terrible idea. Human feelings are not reliable guides. Many things we often feel like doing are not good or right. That's why we have rules.

No rules = chaos.

What if there were no consistent rules or laws? Imagine what it would be like if we all did just what we felt like doing. This is what happens in a famous novel called *Lord of the Flies* by William Golding. The story begins with a plane crashing on a deserted jungle island. Surviving the crash are a group of school boys all under 12 years old with no adults to supervise or take care of them. A few boys look around them and see that order is needed, at least for sanitation and to keep a signal fire going. These boys try to establish some basic rules. But the others don't want those boring old rules. They only want to have fun. They shed their clothes and paint their faces. They make weapons to hunt and kill animals for the blood and thrill of it. They mount a hideous wild boar's head on a tall stake like a trophy where it is covered with flies. Rumors of a monstrous beast spread fear, suspicion, and panic. In the middle of all this chaos murder is committed, and after that no one is safe. When they are finally rescued and the remaining boys see adults dressed in clean clothes and acting civilized, they suddenly realize what they have become and are terribly ashamed.

Without God's rules, human beings end up behaving badly and there are negative consequences for everybody. History is full of evidence of how this can happen. Scriptures relate story after story of governments and peoples who reject God's rules and perish. Think about the Ten Commandments and what our society would be like without these foundational rules. We would no doubt see more of what happened in *Lord of the Flies.* Lawlessness and evil could easily overpower order and good.

This is the direction our country, along with the rest of the world, seems to be moving. Some of today's customs, public policies, and laws are not in harmony with God's unchanging laws. Several of these bad ideas and practices concern chastity and procreation. Here are some specific examples: In America it is legal for pregnant mothers to abort their unborn babies if they don't want them. Courts are also ruling that parents have no right to interfere in the education of their children. Young teenagers are given bad information, contraceptives, and abortions without their parents' knowledge. Keep your ears open and you will hear of more unsound rules being adopted that encourage and excuse sexual immorality. You might say all this is very bad manners. Abandoning God's standard only leads to trouble.

The question for young Latter-day Saints is: Will we follow the world or will we follow God? Will we choose unchastity or chastity, bad sexual manners or good sexual manners? Because these are opposites, we can't do both at the same time. We have to prefer one way of life over another, encouraging one while

Will we choose good sexual manners or bad?

rejecting the other. One way will be supported while the other way will be harmed. There's no way around it. We make the choice, individually and as a society.

Some believe that the bad things people do in private don't hurt anybody. Wrong! The things we do, good and bad, right and wrong, affect ourselves and others. Unchastity results in private and public disasters. Some of these include babies born to unwed mothers, abortions, the spreading of sexually transmitted diseases, the breaking up of homes and families, and even the strain on public funds. Our government spends a huge amount of our tax dollars dealing with problems caused by bad sexual manners.

For various reasons, many who are unchaste want to spread unchastity to everyone else. They are getting their way in our culture, bit by bit. This is how Satan works. He introduces lies and temptations so gradually and cleverly that people don't realize the damage being done.

So let's get this straight. Rules for sexual manners come from God. But plenty of people are forgetting, ignoring, or rebelling against His rules and making up their own like the boys in *Lord of the Flies.* They are taking God-given sexuality and twisting and distorting it for their own purposes. This is like taking a nice yellow banana and smashing it into a spoiled, mushy mess. But it doesn't have to be spoiled for you. Let's clear the dark, overgrown path and shed some light on all of this so we can see things as they really are.

Unchastity is spreading like a disease.

All children are born into this world innocent about sexual things. As they mature, children should be taught by their parents in spoken and unspoken ways the right attitudes and information about human sexuality. Just like a baby is gradually taught the proper way to feed himself at the table—from fingers, to spoon, and then to knife, fork, and napkin—young people should be taught proper sexual manners at age-appropriate times. When sexual feelings begin to develop, young people who have been taught correctly will want to participate in what they've seen other couples do, such as talk to each other, sit by each other, walk side-by-side, hold hands. And they'll know there is a right time, right place, and right person for these and other appropriate demonstrations of affection. They'll use restraint because they'll want to stay within God's boundaries.

Sexual manners are taught and learned.

Some people think good sexual manners will just come naturally. This is not so. Young people have to be taught and learn correct principles about their sexuality. If not, they'll pick up the bad sexual manners coming from the jungle around them and may find themselves being chased by that elephant.

It isn't hard to see how good sexual manners fit into God's plan to make us perfect like Him. Think of all the Christ-like attributes we can learn by choosing to be chaste. As we obey God's law of chastity because we love Him, we can learn unselfishness, humility, patience, reliance on the Lord, listening to the Holy Ghost, and more. These are all traits that make us not just good, but holy, fit for Heavenly Father's gift of eternal life. Striving to have good sexual manners in a world that often resembles a lawless jungle, while relying on Christ, is one of many ways we can show love for Heavenly Father and develop spiritually.

Good sexual manners fit into God's plan.

5

Loincloths, Etc.

– modesty and chastity –

Tarzan wears only a strip of animal skin tied around his hips. When he meets Jane, she is wearing a long skirt, a blouse with a high neck and long sleeves, and high button shoes, like girls wore 100 years ago. Just like these fictional characters from the original Tarzan books by Edgar Rice Burroughs, we wear clothing that fits our time, place, and activities. For instance, the way Tarzan dressed was fine for his active life in the jungle where he was the only human being around. But a loincloth definitely wouldn't work for boy in an American junior high school.

Besides choosing clothes that are appropriate, we choose clothes that reflect our beliefs. When we talk about clothes we can also talk about styles, modesty, and chastity. God's plan is the thread that ties these things together.

Styles come and go. One example is flared pants. In the 1970s young people were wearing them, calling them bellbottoms. Then they went out of style in the '80s and everybody wore jeans cut close to their ankles. For a long time there were no bellbottoms anywhere. Thirty years later, people are wearing bellbottoms again and calling them flares. If only they hadn't

tossed out their old bellbottoms! Styles don't matter very much. What matters is if our clothes are clean, modest, and appropriate. Church leaders have said it's okay to go ahead and enjoy some of the styles of the day as long as we don't go to extremes.

What about modesty? In church we talk a lot about wearing modest clothes. Leaders want to make sure girls dress in a way that is respectful to themselves and not purposely tempting to the boys. Also, it's a good idea for young people to practice dressing in ways that prepare them for the temple. Of course there are times when we wear clothes that are appropriate for a particular activity, such as swimming and sports, that are not appropriate at other times. Even then, we can be relatively modest in our choices.

What about modesty?

If immodest clothing is a problem, it's a good idea to find out why. Once we know why we, or someone else, is dressing inappropriately, we'll know better how to change or help. There are lots of reasons people dress in immodest or extreme ways. One reason is they just don't realize they are dressing immodestly. Maybe they haven't been shown how to present themselves in a respectful way. Modesty is another thing that has to be taught and learned. Another reason is because certain immodest styles might happen to be trendy; it's easy to get caught up in current fashions without thinking them through. On the other hand, some people dress in outlandish ways on purpose, to get attention. Others may actually want to cause others to feel uncomfortable and embarrassed.

None of the above reasons for dressing immodestly are necessarily about chastity. How a person dresses may, or may not, have something to do with being chaste. Chastity begins with what's going on inside us, in our hearts and minds. Dressing immodestly is unchaste if it is done to create lust in oneself or others. Lust is sexual desire outside of God's moral boundaries. It is about using sexual feelings in a totally selfish way and is a sin.

But there is much more to modesty than the clothes we wear. Our language can be modest or immodest, chaste or unchaste, too. In *For the Strength of Youth,* young people are reminded not to swear, use vulgar words or gestures, or participate in jokes about unchastity. It's too bad that there is inappropriate talk in our media and in people's everyday conversations. Sex and sexuality are topics that require modesty and respect.

There's more to modesty than clothes.

How about how we sit, walk, or dance? Our positions and movements can be modest or immodest, too. They can be chaste or unchaste, depending on our motives. If you keep yourself open to the whispering of the Holy Ghost, you will know when you are out-of-bounds in how you carry and express yourself.

And there's more. Technology has opened up a jungleful of new ways to be immodest and unchaste in our language and behaviors. Digital cameras, cell phones, cell phone cameras, text messaging, instant messaging, internet chat rooms, web cams, and blogs can be used inappropriately. Some young people tend to think it's okay to be immodest and unchaste in cyberspace, as if the rules don't apply unless you're interacting in person. They forget that all these technological tricks have real people doing real things behind them. Bad words and bad behavior are just as real and just as wrong on a text message or web cam as they are face to face. Young people should

Wrong is just as wrong in cyberspace as it is face to face.

know that participating in these types of activities is not only immodest, unchaste, and immoral, but illegal. It's against the law to produce and distribute sexual material involving children or teenagers, even if the pictures are of yourself.

We've talked about why people might be immodest. Now let's talk about why people are modest. They might be modest because of the good examples around them. They might do so because they are afraid of disobeying their parents, leaders, or God. But what is the best reason to be modest and chaste, inside and out? The celestial reason to be modest and chaste is because we love Heavenly Father and know He loves us. We understand how valuable we are as children of God. We know that our bodies are His creations and that our clothes are meant to dignify them. We follow Jesus' example of obeying Heavenly Father out of love for Him.

It's the *why* that's important.

There is no such thing as a complete list of rules about modesty in appearance, speech, and conduct. But here is the main rule: listen to the Spirit. It will safely guide you through our worldly jungle of temptations and misinformation about modesty and chastity. If you get started on a wrong path, the Holy Ghost will let you know in a small, quiet way, and help you get back on the right path.

A little more about God's love. This spiritual resource is not only the best way to understand the need for modest and chaste behavior, it is also the best way to understand your true worth.

Too often our feelings of self worth are like a yo-yo. They go up on a good hair day and down on a bad hair day. They go up when we buy new clothes and down when our clothes feel all wrong. They go up when we get noticed by others and down when we are less popular. They go up when we do well and down when we make mistakes. They go up when we have a boyfriend or girlfriend and down when we get dumped. This is what scriptures call being tossed to and fro and it's no fun.

This is where God's love comes in. There is one way to enjoy a steady flow of good feelings about ourselves no matter what. This involves praying often about our immeasurable, unchangeable, enormous worth to Heavenly Father and His Son, and Their perfect, unceasing love for us. If we pray often about who we are and how much Heavenly Father and Jesus love and value us, soon the Holy Ghost will confirm that it's true. As a result, we'll value ourselves (and all others) highly, as we should, in a spiritual way. We'll feel good about ourselves even on a bad hair day, wearing totally out-of-style jeans. Not only that, but feeling this love will cause us to want to obey God's laws, including the law of chastity. When we understand God's love for us, we understand why there are rules. We'll want to do good things for the right reasons.

LISTEN TO THE SPIRIT!

One more thought about modesty. Girls should dress and act modestly so as not to appear as if they are trying to encourage sexual feelings in boys. We say "appear" because appearance may be all it is. No matter how a girl dresses—even if she wears a potato sack—somebody may choose to entertain unchaste thoughts about her. But dressing and acting in a way that does not purposely entice others is the least girls can do. This does not mean they have to make themselves unattractive. Each of us has a stewardship from Heavenly Father to care for our appearance and look our best. We are ultimately not responsible for the unchaste thoughts of others. For example, boys should remember that no matter how a girl looks, dresses, or acts, she is a precious daughter of God who deserves to be thought of and treated with the respect every person deserves.

What do you suppose Jesus thinks about people who are immodest or unchaste? Of course he loves them as much as he loves us all. And because he loves them he invites them to return to the right path. That means loving God and valuing themselves as God does, and showing it through modesty and chastity, whether they're wearing the latest designer jeans . . . or a loincloth!

6

Think Before You Swing

– connecting thoughts and agency –

Ever watch those old black-and-white Tarzan movies from the 1930s and '40s? Whenever there's some jungle emergency Tarzan appears high up in a tree. He grabs a rope-like vine. In a series of long smooth motions he swings from one vine to another, through the tall trees, safely above wildly stampeding animals. Finally, he arrives at the scene of the trouble and saves the day.

You might wonder how Tarzan's vines always seem to be so handy. Transjungle vines don't just appear in exactly the right places at exactly the right moments. You can be sure the high-flying Tarzan knows his aerial freeway system backwards and forwards, that he has a plan, that he always thinks before he swings.

Tarzan is a pretty active character, what we'd call an action figure. But if he were a real person and we could see inside his brain, we'd find that all his big daring deeds start with thoughts. Have you ever considered a thought as being a tiny mental action? Many times each day we decide what to think about. Each of those quiet, invisible mental actions leads to attitudes and feelings that could lead to physical behavior.

Generally, thoughts are the rope-like vines that connect our actions. They take us where we want to go. They make us the kind of person we are. There are many kinds of thoughts. Some can be chaste or unchaste, pure or lustful, right or wrong.

A thought is a tiny mental action.

A book called *A Separate Peace* by John Knowles shows the danger of thinking wrong thoughts. Two best friends, Phineas and Gene, are students at a boys' boarding school during a summer term. Phineas is a gifted athlete. Gene is an outstanding student. The two boys make a pact to do a certain daring deed every day. They decide to climb a tall tree by a river and jump off a branch that hangs out over the water, just like Tarzan would do. They each make the dangerous jump successfully every day for weeks. Then one day Phineas suggests they go to the tree when Gene happens to be studying, and a thought pops into Gene's mind. The thought in his mind is that Phineas is trying to keep him from doing well on an upcoming test. As they walk to the tree, the horrible new idea that Phineas is a false friend plays over and over in Gene's mind. Phineas starts climbing first and Gene follows. As Phineas carefully inches out toward the water, Gene finds himself jiggling the branch ever so slightly. At that moment Phineas slips and falls to the ground below, shattering his leg. Gene is devastated, and things only get worse. He learns the hard way that wrong thoughts may lead to bad actions whether we really mean them to or not.

It's a simple concept. Thoughts make the man. You are what you think. As man thinks, so is he. The scriptures call it reaping what we sow. Old sayings like these are repeated through the centuries for a reason: they have proven time and time again to be true.

Bad thoughts may come into our minds uninvited. Or we might choose to think bad thoughts on purpose. But no matter how they get there, we have the power to send them away. We can reject bad thoughts and replace them with good thoughts. The best way to get rid of wrong thoughts is to pray, which we will talk more about in chapter nine. This is a way to use God's gift of agency, or free will. A wise person is very careful about what thoughts fill his mind.

> **It takes effort to think good thoughts.**

It may feel like we can't control our thoughts. But we can. Every healthy person can. Still, it's a big responsibility. It's difficult to always keep our thoughts firm, good, and true. Like water, thoughts can easily flow and puddle in the lowest places. If we don't work at holding right thoughts in our minds, they may end up in the mud. It takes some mental muscle to keep our thoughts flying high, like Tarzan swinging in the trees.

It's very important to make the distinction between things we can't control and things we can control. The way this world is set up, there are some events we can't do much or anything about, things like birth defects, being called names by a bully, being hit by a car when you're innocently walking on the sidewalk, or natural phenomena such as hurricanes or tidal waves. There are also many things that are definitely within our control, things like how we spend our free time, what we wear, what we take into our bodies, how we treat others, and sexual thoughts.

We've talked about thoughts. How about feelings? Remember that sexual feelings are part of God's plan. As young people grow up, it is likely that they'll experience them to some degree and feel curious. They may want to ask questions and learn about them from a trusted source. That's fine. The trick is not to take these involuntary feelings too seriously. A movement, a sensation, the fit of your clothes, or an image you happen to see might trigger sexual feelings. This is true for both boys and girls, but even more so for boys. Don't be concerned about them. They don't mean anything except that you are a healthy person with God-given sexual feelings that will be useful and enjoyable when you get married to a person of the opposite sex.

Sexual feelings are part of God's plan.

Involuntary sexual feelings develop gradually. They come and go. But sexual feelings can also be purposely stimulated. This is not okay except between husband and wife. Some people in our modern-day jungle of bad manners and ideas are saying that feelings can't be helped and all feelings are good. This is not true. We have to make decisions about feelings. We have to ask ourselves, is this feeling right or wrong? Is it appropriate or inappropriate? Is it chaste or unchaste? The Spirit can let us know.

Is there a link between thoughts and feelings? Yes. Sometimes the feeling comes first, such as when your stomach growls so you think of food. Other times the thought comes first, such as when you see a food commercial on TV and you suddenly feel hungry. Thoughts and feelings work both ways, and both thoughts and feelings can be schooled or controlled. A good rule of thumb is *if you shouldn't do it, you shouldn't think or feel it.* Each of us has the responsibility to seek the Spirit of the Lord through prayer to help us choose good thoughts and feelings.

Feelings can be chaste or unchaste.

We could call any premature, out-of-place, or excessive sexual thoughts and feelings *temptations*. Temptations lead to more thoughts, feelings, and actions that are out of bounds. Satan is very good at disguising temptations. His goal is to make them look good and right instead of bad and wrong. He is having his way on a grand scale in the world today.

Problems come when healthy developing sexual thoughts and feelings get overstimulated, become troublesome, or take the wrong path. You can avoid or correct those problems. The best way to do this is by turning back to the Lord in your mind with an obedient heart full of love for Heavenly Father. Knowing the truth about sexuality, praying always, and listening carefully to the Holy Ghost will dispel temptations.

We've talked about our culture as a jungle of bad ideas. Today, sex and sexuality are overemphasized and distorted. Is it possible for young people to keep right thoughts in their minds at such a time and place? Yes. You have been given the agency to do this. Agency, or the freedom to choose, is essential. Without agency we couldn't be tested, we couldn't learn from experience, and we couldn't progress. It's really quite a wonderful opportunity to gird up our "loincloths" and choose which side we're on.

Even in a jungle you have agency.

As you prepare to someday go to the temple, you should know that you will be required to make sacred covenants with the Lord to keep not only your physical actions but your thoughts and desires within God's boundaries. You can start now. The Spirit of the Lord will help you sort out your thoughts and feelings and choose only those that are appropriate, healthy, and wholesome. Like Tarzan, you can learn to think before you swing.

7

No Time for Monkey Business

– getting acquainted with the opposite sex –

Like Tarzan and Jane, healthy young people of the opposite sex who have been taught correctly tend to pair off, and that's wonderful and good when the time is right. Ideally, parents are good examples of male and female roles. They teach their children in spoken and unspoken ways about their developing sexual thoughts and feelings. Healthy young people should learn almost unconsciously that it is, or will be, natural and right to find they are attracted in a special way to the opposite sex. After all, it's what happens in earnest when a man and a woman promise themselves to each other in marriage. It's pleasant and even exciting to be especially noticed by someone or to notice someone you find interesting. But because you are developing sexually, and sex is a serious thing, this is no time for monkey business. Let's talk about some things you should know.

Now is the time to learn in social ways how boys are different and interesting to girls and how girls are different and interesting to boys. In group settings like school, Young Men and Young Women activities, dances, parties, sports events, and perhaps other chaperoned get-togethers, boys and girls can interact

socially and get acquainted. These kinds of activities give you several years in safe settings to gain confidence in your own masculinity or femininity.

Chaperoned means adults are present and supervising.

While it's natural for young people to find someone of the opposite sex interesting and begin to develop special feelings for them, this is not the time to seriously pair off. The Spirit will tell you to be lighthearted about such feelings and not to overthink them. Chances are you will find several people you especially like in these early years. This is how you learn about different personalities.

Young people often want to be popular, to feel noticed and accepted by other young people. It's exciting to be admired. Having a special someone might give a young person a feeling of security and belonging. You may think you need a boyfriend or girlfriend in order to be somebody and feel good about yourself. But here you need to remember that truly reliable good feelings of self worth don't come from other people. They come from God. The truth is, you don't need an admirer to feel loved; you have a Heavenly Father. You don't need a boyfriend or girlfriend to make you feel valued; you have the Savior. You don't need a special constant companion; you have the Holy Ghost. You can get all the good and secure feelings you need from the Godhead, and now is a perfect time to practice this.

You can know you are of great worth without a boyfriend or girlfriend.

Remember also that you can control what you think and feel. Sometimes it is just the power of suggestion or peer pressure that causes young people to pair off. Maybe you hear from a friend that somebody has a crush on you. Wow! But here's what you might not realize: you don't have to like someone just because they like you. When you know you can control your thoughts and feelings, and when you value yourself as a cherished child of God, you feel free to choose if you will like someone specially or not.

There are good reasons to put off having an exclusive boyfriend or girlfriend until you are older. When too-young couples spend a lot of time together they are more likely to become too dependent on each other, which stops their social progress. Modern technology makes it even easier to become too personally involved through email, texting, webcamming, instant messaging, or other online social networks. Young people may also become too familiar with each other physically. When familiarity starts too soon, that elephant is more likely to stampede out of God's boundaries. Physical intimacy gets mixed up with immature emotions and can lead to bad decisions.

It is easy to jump to conclusions about physical attraction and decide it means love. But remember how elephants can't jump or they'll crush their bones? That's how it is with physical attraction and love too. We mustn't jump to conclusions about serious things or we'll hurt ourselves and others. Just because you are physically attracted to someone does not mean you love them. There is a big distance to travel between physical attraction and real love. That's why it's important to be lighthearted about romance for now. Physical attraction is the beginning of sexual feelings which must wait until the proper time and place, much closer to marriage, when you

Physical attraction and love are two different things.

can prepare to share those feelings with the person you marry.

The jungle we live in today spreads the dangerous idea that love and sexual attraction are the same thing. It says if you feel attracted to someone in that way, you must love them, when really, sexual feelings just tell you your body is working. It also spreads the equally dangerous but opposite idea that love and sex need not be connected. It says you don't have to love someone to be physically intimate with them. Many people today want intimate physical relations to be a leisure activity with no responsibilities, as casual as sharing a game of tennis or an ice cream cone. They do not want to think about commitment, marriage, children, or family. They just want to gratify their sexual desires then and there. This is not what Heavenly Father intends. In many ways the world around us is taking a private, beautiful, essential part of life and monkeying around with it. These are all things you now need to know even before you're old enough to date.

Some people turn physical intimacy into a casual activity with no responsibilities.

What about dating? Dating can be fun, but it also has some serious aspects to it. Dating is serious because it requires chastity at a time when you are developing sexually and finding an interest in the opposite sex. Dating is serious because it leads to the biggest step in your life: marriage, which includes the fulfillment of sexual intimacy. Dating is especially serious business today because love, sex, and procreation are being monkeyed with in our modern-day jungle. In preparation, you need to know the when, what, why, and how of proper dating.

Dating has a serious side.

The When of Dating

LDS youth have been counseled by Church leaders to hold off dating until the age of sixteen. Even then it is wise to date in groups of couples. At college age, or after serving a mission, young people should start single dating in earnest in search of their future husband or wife.

There are many reasons why this is good counsel. For instance, holding off dating until you're sixteen can protect you from becoming too dependent, or too familiar too soon with the opposite sex, as mentioned earlier. Dating in groups after sixteen can also provide opportunities to develop social skills, and is a fun, relaxed way to get to know different personalities. By college age you should have the confidence and skills needed for single dating and have an idea about the kind of person you will want for a mate. These and others are good reasons, but you can obey this counsel for the best reason: because you love Heavenly Father.

The What of Dating

Let's talk about the exciting time when dating is not only appropriate but necessary in order to find a wonderful future spouse. What is the definition of dating? What exactly is a real date? An eleven-year-old girl was asked what she thought a real date was and she shrugged her shoulders. "Maybe just hanging out?" she asked. That's not the right answer. Dating means spending unchaperoned time appropriately with someone of the opposite sex. Here is a scenario of what a real date should be like:

What does a real date look like?

Tarzan calls Jane several days in advance and asks her to go to a play, a basketball game, a concert, a dance, a movie, out to eat, bike riding, or ice skating—you get the idea—some activity in a public place. Jane thinks it over for a minute and then says something like, "Sure, I'd like to go," or "No, but thanks for asking." If she says yes, then on the appointed day at the appointed time Tarzan arrives to pick up Jane. Jane is all ready to go and the couple leaves for their date. They do whatever appropriate activity Tarzan had in mind when he called Jane. Tarzan pays any expenses, takes Jane home, and walks her to her door where the two say their thank-yous and part. Now that's a real date.

We need to define a real date because young people today tend to do a lot of "hanging out" rather than real dating. Hanging out is when any number of boys and any number of girls casually gather to talk, eat, watch movies, play games and sports, or participate in other activities. It is not group dating. For a group date, Tarzan still singles out one girl and asks her to go somewhere special with him as they join other couples. You may be asking, what's wrong with hanging out? Well, it can be a fun way to get acquainted with members of the opposite sex. But it becomes a problem when it takes the place of important real dating.

In a real date, the boy takes the lead.

We also need to define a real date because nowadays Jane is asking Tarzan out as much or more than Tarzan is asking Jane. This doesn't match up with the way God made male and female. Young men should step up to their manly role and do most of the asking out on dates. This requires some effort and courage. There is always the possibility that the girl might say no—ouch! No one likes to be rejected. But this is the risk a boy has to take. Young women have a different role. They should be friendly, encouraging, and patient. And if a girl gets asked out and doesn't want to go, she needs to be as kind as possible in turning the young man down.

Whether you're a guy or a girl, there are pros and cons to this set-up. Boys have to do some planning and take the risk of asking a girl out. Girls have to be patient, may not get asked out, or may have the unpleasant task of saying no occasionally. But real dating—the male taking the lead—is another one of those customs, backed by true principles, that we shouldn't monkey around with.

The Why of Dating

A real date has more to it than just going out with someone of the opposite sex. It helps develop your personality and is good practice for learning how to get along with an opposite-sex person. It is also good practice for the time when a young man gets up the courage to ask a young woman to marry him, and she makes the choice. Even beyond that, real dating is symbolic of proper gender roles and traditions in marriage that fit God's plan. Tarzan has to get up the courage to ask Jane out, treat her courteously, and pay the expenses. This helps him learn how to be a good husband. Both Tarzan and Jane have a chance to learn how to interact socially one-on-one, which they will have to know how to do in marriage. And Jane gets the chance to dress and act modestly and see that Tarzan especially cares about her as a whole person. She is looking forward to being a virtuous mother who will need a devoted and trustworthy husband and father for her children.

This may sound old-fashioned and politically incorrect,

but it's generally the best way and the way most in keeping with nature and God's laws. In proper dating, boys and girls are practicing their natural gender roles.

The How of Dating

Often young people want the rules for physical contact while dating written out clearly and concisely on a sheet of paper. They don't like adults hinting around at what they're not supposed to do. But there is really no such thing as a comprehensive list for chaste conduct. A good list is helpful, but no list is complete, not in our bad-mannered jungle today. Things are happening so fast that decent people cannot keep up. As a result, however conscientious we try to be, any list we use now will have something missing on it that can trip us up unawares.

You need much more than a list of rules. You need the Spirit.

That's another way Satan uses his cunning. It's like one of those jungle rope traps. You're walking along without a care in the world and all of a sudden you're hanging from a tree upside down. It's a big surprise, but it's even more surprising if you've forgotten or haven't realized you've been walking around in a very dangerous place. Still, there's no need to worry if you're prepared.

When you go on a jungle safari, your chances of enjoyment and safety are much better if you have the proper knowledge and equipment. So what do you need most for successful dating? You guessed it: the Holy Ghost. No matter

Don't forget the world can be a dangerous place.

how many rules, booklets, lessons, and scriptures there are about chastity, you need the Spirit to whisper obedience, truth, warnings, comfort, strength, and resolve. The Holy Ghost is what will truly keep your thoughts, feelings, and actions within God's boundaries, and it is up to each young person to get to know that quiet voice.

The dating years are a great time to grow spiritually. Both boys and girls should present themselves appropriately as the male or female Heavenly Father made them. They can learn to love God, to feel His love, and to obey His Law of chastity in spirit, thought, and deed, because of that love.

When you're on a date, the knowledge that you and the person you are with are cherished children of Heavenly Father will cause you to treat each other with great respect. Staying close to the Lord is the best way to keep sexual feelings developing wholesomely. With the Holy Ghost as your guide, you can enjoy years of fun dating and look forward to temple marriage with someone of the opposite sex just right for you and the wonderful possibility of a family. And that's no monkey business.

8

Wild Elephant!

– misuses of the procreative power –

Ever heard an elephant joke? They were really popular in the 1960s. In those days people were always telling elephant jokes and making up new ones. They were really silly. Get ready. Here are a few:

Q: What time is it when an elephant sits on your fence?
A: Time to get a new fence.

Q: How do elephants communicate?
A: On the elephone.

Q: What did Tarzan say when he saw the elephants come over the hill?
A. "Here come the elephants over the hill." (Keep going. The joke isn't over.)

Q: What did Tarzan say when the elephants were wearing sunglasses?
A: Nothing. He didn't recognize them.

Q: What time is it when ten elephants are chasing you?
A. Ten to one!

All joking aside, even one multi-ton wild elephant chasing you would not be funny at all. You'd run as fast as you could. You'd be gasping for breath. You'd be scared to look behind you. Your heart would be pounding out of your chest. Or maybe you'd be paralyzed with fear. In that case you'd freeze in your tracks, staring in disbelief as the monstrously huge animal stampeded closer and closer.

An eight-ton elephant chasing you is no joke.

One last elephant joke:

Q: What's the squishy stuff between elephants' toes?
A: Slow natives.

Today's wild version of sexuality is like a stampeding elephant and we are the natives of this world. Every one of us is in danger of meeting the fate of slow natives when it comes to wrong attitudes, ideas, and conduct. If we don't get the facts straight about chastity and sexual morality according to the gospel truth, and seek the Spirit always, every one of us could end up, well, elephant toe jam.

The following sections outline some of the ways human sexuality is stampeding dangerously out of control and why this is wrong and harmful in many ways. We know from The Book of Mormon that there are many ways people can commit sin, so many that they cannot all be named (Mosiah 4:29). But here are some you should know about. As always, the Holy Ghost can be your guide as to the truthfulness of what follows.

Sex for Kids?

A fictional movie tells how a man has invented the Hula Hoop and can't get anyone to pay attention to his idea. That's because all he shows them is a line drawing of a simple circle while saying, "You know, for kids!" Incredibly, some people say the same thing about sex: You know, for kids! Without thinking things through, they teach their radical ideas about sex and sexuality to children and teenagers from kindergarten through high school. They do not care about childhood innocence and what parents want their children to learn. They reject God and His law of chastity. Schools and other organizations are not only teaching children and teenagers wrong ideas about sexuality, but also encouraging acting out, calling it "safe sex." This sex education is dead wrong. Here's why:

Sex is not for kids. Period.

1. Sex is not for kids.

2. It is parents who should teach their children about sexual matters.

3. School is for academic subjects like reading and math. Sex and sexuality are not school subjects.

4. Unchastity is not safe. It hurts people emotionally, physically, and spiritually. It destroys families. By "safe sex" people really mean "go ahead,

> try anything and everything; just use contraceptives so that no one gets pregnant or gets a disease." This false teaching endangers the health, safety, and well-being of young people and their posterity. Of course sexual relations are only safe between a healthy, chaste, opposite-sex, faithful couple.

Obviously, some adults are all mixed up and want to mix kids up, too. Sex education is a big part of a modern movement to dismiss God and spread human sexuality far beyond God's boundaries. Unchastity is taught and encouraged through library books, text books, videos, lessons, workshops, flyers, booklets, school newspapers, assemblies, and free contraceptives. Spreading inappropriate information and lies about sex and sexuality to minors is inexcusable. It is a form of child sexual abuse. It is too bad that much of our society is not only allowing it, but encouraging it.

Some adults are all mixed up.

The Abortion Connection

You might wonder what abortion has to do with stampeding sexuality. In 1973 abortion was legalized by the U.S. Supreme Court. This was a tragic decision. From then on any woman could legally have a doctor kill, remove, and discard her healthy growing unborn baby without a medical reason. Some have compared an abortion to the removal of a cancerous tumor, as if a developing human being is a disease.

People are still trying hard to reverse this very bad court decision. But tragically, since then, approximately 50 million unborn babies have been purposely destroyed in this nation simply because they were not wanted or valued. A baby is aborted about every thirty seconds. How terrible! If these unborn babies had been left alone in their mothers' wombs, most all of them would have been safely born, given a name, and grown to adulthood like everyone else. You can see that this practice willfully devalues and destroys human life when it is most vulnerable and defenseless.

Needless abortion has been given other names to make it sound positive, such as "pro-choice" or "reproductive freedom." Don't be fooled. In using these clever labels, people deny that human beings are perfectly free to choose whether or not to have sexual relations in the first place. They deny that pregnancy may be a very real consequence of sexual relations and that abstinence (refraining from sexual relations) *always* prevents pregnancy. Abortion activists also push the idea that pregnant women have the right to be in charge of their bodies. But this denies the fact that when a woman is pregnant there is another human life besides her own involved. Many women have been led to believe the lies pushed by those who do not value human life. And many, who make the mistake of having an abortion, later realize how terribly wrong it was. They wish they had let their babies be born.

Abortion has become popular because it is a way for people to escape the responsibilities that come with sexual intercourse. Killing the unborn is actually practiced as a form of birth control by many in our culture today. Now you can see how abortion is connected to out-of-bounds sexuality. Because of legalized abortion, people know they can be unchaste with anyone anytime without worrying about the possibility of parenthood. If they happen to get pregnant, they can just go to a clinic and have the life terminated.

Abortion is a way to escape responsibility.

Abortion for convenience is one of the many ways our society now separates the sexual act from its primary purpose: procreation, which includes motherhood, fatherhood, and family. It is evidence of a society that would rather kill a baby than require that it be born and placed with a grateful adoptive couple. It shows how selfish adult pleasures are valued above innocent human life, God, and His laws.

The Center for Disease Control reports that at least 80% of all abortions are performed on unmarried women. (Rape victims amount to less than 1%.) From this statistic we know that most of the women who get abortions are unmarried and unchaste. Don't forget that this also means their male partners were unchaste, too. There goes that dangerous stampeding elephant.

The Pornography Plague

What is pornography? It is any material produced with intent to stir up lust. Lust is out-of-bounds sexual thoughts and feelings. President Gordon B. Hinckley referred to pornography as "sleazy filth."

Do not confuse pornography with positive romantic or artistic material that is worthwhile and in good taste. Pornography is explicit material used to intentionally exploit physical desires in people, disconnected from love and marriage, in order to make money. By contrast, the wholesome material we find in classic art and literature treats these things in a modest and respectful way, connecting them with the rightness of chastity, responsibility, and traditional marriage.

Pornography itself isn't new. What's new is the huge amount of it being produced and the way we allow it in our society. Not long ago this sordid material was confined to adults-only places like certain bookstores and theaters. Now because of modern technology and lowered standards, it takes many forms and is found in many places. It marches uninvited into our homes, workplaces, libraries, and schools by way of TV and the internet. It has become a multi-billion dollar industry. Talk about a stampede!

Pornography is vulgar material intended to incite lust.

There are reasons we have so much pornography besides the money involved. One reason is because some people in charge have rejected God and make decisions for our country as if His law of chastity is not important. We know that without God there is no objective or reliable standard for sexual conduct. Another reason we have pornography is the popular idea that people should be free to engage in whatever sexual behaviors they want to as long as they are legal. This is a bad idea. Many acts are now legal but remain immoral and harmful, such as adultery and convenient abortion.

Generally, our society is failing to take the plague of pornography seriously enough. Most do not understand what it does to people. Remember, our sexual identities are meant to be used under one circumstance only, that is, between a kind and loving husband and wife. When the sexual drive is misused people get hurt. People are getting hurt by pornography. Everyone needs to stop and think about what's wrong with pornography.

Pornography hurts people.

Here are eight simple reasons why pornography is evil and harmful:

1. It makes cheap and public what should be special and private between a husband and wife.

2. It makes children of God seem like inanimate toys or objects that do not deserve respect.

3. It warps people's perceptions of reality, proper sexuality, and true affection.

4. It is dangerously addictive like a drug, some say worse than drugs.

5. It has been shown to lead to sex crimes.

6. It is destructive to individuals, marriages, families, and communities.

7. It causes people to break all ten of the Ten Commandments.

8. It takes forms that are unspeakably depraved and deadly.

Have you ever played chess? If you have, you know that there are several different kinds of pieces on the board that must be moved differently. The easiest pieces to learn about are the pawns. There are eight pawns on each side, more than any other kind of piece. They can only move in the simplest ways, such as one square forward per turn. Pawns are considered the least powerful and most disposable pieces on the board, existing to be used for the benefit of the other pieces. Where pornography is concerned, the person viewing it is like a pawn, being exploited so others can get gain. You need not be anybody's pawn.

We've said that pornography is extremely addictive. You've heard of drug addictions that cause addicts to do anything to get a fix. Drug dealers seek out potential addicts hoping to get them hooked. They see addicts as an easy source of money. It's the same with pornography dealers. Billions of dollars are being made because pornography is addictive. Addicts keep coming back for more. The people who make pornography become wealthy by finding lifetime customers, the younger the better. One specialist, Dr. Matthew Hedelius, helps free people from this terrible addiction. His clients are most often male, age eleven and up. He said, "We tell people that if you don't get this problem taken care of, it'll kill you."

> **People make pornography to get money.**

How can anybody overlook such a big dangerous elephant?

Bad Dates

It's fun to remember favorite lines from movies. There's a short one worth quoting in the first Indiana Jones movie when

Indy is about to eat a date from a bowl of fruit. He throws the fruit up to catch it in his mouth. Suddenly, his friend snatches it in midair and directs Indy's surprised gaze to the monkey he has just discovered dead with the half-eaten poisoned fruit in its grasp. "Bad dates," is all he says. There are other kinds of bad dates, the kind when guys and girls spend time together and things go terribly wrong. We cannot list them all, but here are some you should know about.

Dating is not for sex.

One way dates go wrong is when young unmarried couples become too familiar physically. They may be very fond of each other and committed to their relationship, but this does not give them license to break the law of chastity. You know from the previous chapter that dating is a time to get to know a person in all ways except sexually. The law of chastity commands us to wait for physical intimacy until marriage when a couple makes a covenant between each other and God.

Here, let's get our terms straight. When unmarried couples have sexual intercourse it is called fornication. When a person has sexual intercourse with many people it is called promiscuity. When married people have sexual intercourse with someone other than their spouse it is called adultery. These are forms of sexual sin.

When the law of chastity is broken, it is both the young man and young woman's fault. However, boys need to be aware of their responsibility concerning their sexual drive. Young men today often think it is the girl's job to keep them in check. This is incorrect. Latter-day Saint young men hold the priesthood along with the key to the power of procreation. Therefore, they have a two-fold responsibility to obey the law of chastity. While Jane must use her agency to be modest in her dress and careful in her conduct, Tarzan must realize he is totally responsible for his own behavior, too. He must also know that breaking the law of chastity carries with it certain physical changes and possible consequences for the girl that are nonexistent for the boy, such as pregnancy. This ought to make boys especially careful how they behave toward girls.

Another kind of bad date is when young people get together, not because they know or are fond of each other, but for the sole purpose of physical intimacy. Names for this conduct are NCMO (pronounced nicmo), meaning "non-committal make-out" or "friends with benefits." This behavior turns people into objects, as if they are enacting pornography. It is casual and crude treatment of oneself and others.

Some young people who act out sexually claim that technically they are still virgins. They say this because they have acted out in ways other than normal sexual intercourse. But deep down they know that any out-of-bounds conduct is not virtuous, pure, or chaste at all. You should know that society used to recognize the danger of young people getting involved sexually. In fact, laws still exist, but are not being enforced, that prohibit sexual relations between minors.

> **If you play around with sexual feelings someone is going to get hurt.**

Still another very bad date is when one person takes advantage of another for sexual gratification. Forcing anyone sexually in any way or degree is a crime. Despite today's environment of sexual freedom, some sexual crimes are still taken very seriously and strictly punished by law. This is one of those. Males are usually the perpetrators of date-related misdemeanors and felonies. The law recognizes that boys are usually stronger and bigger than girls, and can easily get their way. Boys from all backgrounds are found guilty of this behavior.

This problem has increased because of the bad-mannered jungle we live in. Boys, especially, are easily influenced by sexual material. They can be lured into pornography and become preoccupied with sex. Such a young man becomes desensitized to the Spirit. He comes to value the sexual sensations he experiences above the protests, modesty, chastity, and safety of his date.

> **Forcing anyone sexually *in any way or degree* is a crime.**

Girls can fall into this trap, too. They can be influenced by their friends, novels, magazines, movies, and pornography. They can become predatory, seducing unsuspecting boys. But usually girls become victims. A girl who badly wants a boyfriend may allow herself to be emotionally manipulated. She may make the mistake of giving in physically by degrees in order to get or keep a boyfriend. Every girl needs to know that any boy who attempts to use her to fulfill sexual fantasies or manipulate her in any other way—mentally, spiritually, or emotionally—does not truly care about her. She should walk away.

Some boys (and some girls, too) often have a way with words. They know how to talk girls into doing things the girls know are wrong. Every girl should watch out for any boy who pays her overly flattering compliments, professes to think exactly the same as she does, centers all their interactions around himself, rationalizes breaking the rules for chastity, or abuses her

Watch out for those bad dates.

in any way, including verbally and psychologically. The same goes for boys. Both young women and young men should know that this kind of treatment is as unacceptable in dating as it is in marriage. A good husband and wife treat one another with unselfishness and respect. Each is gentle, patient, loving, and giving. There is no coercion or manipulation taking place.

Masturbation Misconceptions

For decades now, people have been saying quite publicly that masturbation (sexual self-stimulation) is normal and natural, even healthy, and that everybody does it. This is not true.

Our bodies are a stewardship from Heavenly Father.

People often justify this behavior by referring to the behavior of babies and small children who unashamedly touch themselves. But this is not what we define as masturbation. Little children do not know about sex and are not accountable. As children grow up they learn it is bad manners to touch their private parts in that way. It is a different thing when teenagers and grown-ups stimulate themselves on purpose.

Masturbation satisfies sexual urges that are reserved for the marriage relationship. When a person stimulates his own body he is using his God-given procreative power outside God's law of chastity. This behavior is typically done in secret. But of course no one can keep a secret from the Lord.

Think of it this way. Everything belongs to Heavenly Father, even our bodies. Our bodies are like temples. We have a stewardship assignment to treat them with respect and dignity. This does not include activities that rightly make us feel guilty and ashamed. However, proper shame and guilt can actually serve a good purpose. These feelings come from the Spirit. They are red flags that tell us we're doing something wrong.

Young men should know that as their bodies mature, they will have involuntary erections and nocturnal emissions (wet dreams). This is not masturbation. Both boys and girls should know that there is no accountability when involuntary sexual feelings arise. This is a natural function of their physical bodies letting them know that it is maturing and working properly, and that procreation is a possibility. Remember, young people, especially boys, can become sexually aroused by practically anything. Some are more easily aroused than others. Different situations and different times may also have an effect. Both boys and girls should know not to give any serious thought to involuntary sexual feelings. Just let them go, be grateful to Heavenly Father for your healthy body, and pray for the Spirit.

> **Masturbation is not what sexual feelings are for.**

Masturbation, however, is unacceptable. It can become addictive and interfere with healthy sexual development. Pornography caters to this practice which can easily escalate into more destructive behaviors, such as homosexuality. Watch out for that wild elephant!

The Gay Lie

Sexual attraction between male and female is now often called heterosexuality. Of course we shouldn't need a name for this. It is God's natural pattern. Every healthy human being is heterosexual. We only need the word heterosexuality because some are behaving homosexually and insisting their behavior is of equal value.

Homosexual behavior is males interacting sexually with other males, or females with other females. Historically, our society has rightly considered these behaviors to be unacceptable and caused by mental illness because they are contrary to nature, harmful to ordered society, and clearly condemned by the Bible (Leviticus 18:22 and 20:13, Romans 1:24-32, 1 Corinthians 6:9-10). Until recently, male homosexual behavior (sodomy) was against the law in all fifty states. Wise men know it is a corrupting practice that tends to spread, including from older males to younger. Our Church leaders have consistently warned against this vice. Now, it is given new names and is stampeding through our culture as if it is respectable and harmless.

Homosexuality has expanded into several more "alternative sexual orientations" and so-called genders. Some of these are termed lesbian, gay, bisexual, transgender, transsexual, and questioning, sometimes referred to as LGBTQ. The terms lesbian and gay, or homosexual, same-sex or same-gender attracted, refer to people who claim they can only relate sexually to persons of their same sex. Bisexual describes people who say they are sexually attracted to both sexes. Transgender individuals allege that they are the opposite sex than their body indicates. Transsexuals insist that they were born with the wrong sex organs and desire to act opposite to what their anatomy indicates; some go so far as to take excess hormones and have doctors perform surgeries that give their bodies the appearance of the opposite sex. Questioning is a newish label being used to describe young people who are considering which one (or more!) of the many alleged sexual orientations they prefer.

Although those who adopt such labels represent a very small percentage of the population, they have become a powerful influence. They use media, entertainment, schools, and legislative action to promote societal acceptance. Activists even demand special new rights such as "gay marriage." They want special protections such as "hate crimes" laws, hoping to punish those who disapprove of their conduct. They attack religion and churches that uphold the Bible. They use the negative term "homophobe," claiming that straight (heterosexual) people are fearful of homosexual people to the point of phobia (mental disease). And yet they use their sexuality in ways that mock God, nature, and reality, endangering themselves, others, and society as a whole.

Anything other than normal heterosexuality between a married couple not only exceeds God's boundaries but tampers with nature.

Here are some of the reasons alternative sexual orientations are wrong:

1. God has made it clear that anything other than proper heterosexuality between husband and wife is unchaste.

2. Sexual behaviors other than heterosexual behavior cannot create life and are therefore false imitations of the real thing, or counterfeits.

3. Alternative sexual behaviors do not match up with nature and reality and can be physically harmful to the human body. The body cannot safely accommodate behaviors such as sodomy.

4. Alternative sexual orientations and behaviors separate sex and sexuality from its primary purpose which is marriage, procreation, and family.

5. Being born male or female has eternal significance. Sexual conduct outside heterosexuality frustrates God's plan for His children.

What about health risks for these individuals? Most people know that promiscuity between opposite sexes spreads a variety of sexually transmitted diseases. But not very many people realize the health risks that come with alternative sexual behaviors. These risks are even more varied and dangerous. For instance, homosexual behavior is connected to a long list of chronic, dangerous, and evenpotentially deadly conditions, illnesses, and diseases. This is true for men acting sexually with men as well as women acting sexually with women, although the list for women is somewhat different than for men. Some of these are domestic violence, substance abuse, mental illness, eating disorders, anal cancer, hepatitis, and HIV/AIDS.

You may have been told that HIV/AIDS is a disease anyone can get through any kind of sexual behavior. This is not true. For instance, a faithful husband and wife will never get HIV/AIDS from their sexual relations.

Are these diseases preventable? Of course they are. We choose what we will do with our bodies. If people obeyed the law of chastity there would be no AIDS or any other sexually transmitted diseases. You need to know, in spite of what you may hear, that what healthy people do with their sexuality is a choice.

What about what is being called same-sex or same-gender attraction, SSA or SGA? These are perhaps softer names for homosexual tendencies which are lustful desires for those of one's own sex. Some say these feelings are out of a person's control, but as we learned in chapter six, unless there is a mental health problem, we are free to choose which thoughts and feelings we will allow and nourish and which we will reject and extinguish. A 1991 Letter from the First Presidency reads, ". . . such thoughts and feelings, regardless of their causes, can and should be overcome."

Homosexual behaviors are extremely risky.

For some people these feelings become troublesome and cause stress. They do not know how to overcome these unwanted feelings. In this case, it is important to find out what is causing them. Remember, proper attitudes toward sex are learned, and wrong attitudes are also learned. Same-sex sexual attraction can be learned, or influenced, by gender confusion, peer abuse, family dysfunction, bad luck with the opposite sex, false information, exposure to pornography, sexual abuse, or some combination of these and other environmental factors. A series of unfortunate experiences can indeed interfere with healthy sexual development. Same-sex sexual attraction can be a symptom of deep problems that need to be resolved. Trained therapists are helping many people with unwanted homosexual attraction overcome their problems with a high rate of success.

Today, in our dangerous jungle of bad information and images, the power of suggestion alone can be enough to interest vulnerable young people in out-of-bounds, or alternative, sexual ideas and behaviors. Our modern environment is playing a significant role in leading people into sexual immorality.

Sexual behavior is a choice.

Now you may be asking, wait a minute, aren't people born that way? The answer is an emphatic no. No one is born gay. The human race is biologically heterosexual. God created Adam and Eve as male and female in order to complement each other.

The only way we know people are gay, lesbian, bisexual, or transgender is if they themselves make it known. There is no biological test or medical diagnosis for alternative sexual orientation. It is self-constructed. It's true that some people have personalities more vulnerable or susceptible to false sexual ideas just like some people may be prone to other weaknesses like alcoholism. But learned ideas and acquired vices are not part of our genetic makeup. People can be corrected and overcome these weaknesses and sins, and many do.

Some people troubled by unwanted same-sex sexual attraction feel they have not chosen these feelings. They do not want this problem and choose to overcome it, even if it is a long and difficult process. Others wrongly decide that the only thing they can do is accept that they are gay/SSA and find others who have done the same. Still others admit that they want to rebel against the traditional order of things. Some of these choose to embrace

Wrong feelings can be made right.

this "identity" and join the LGBT community as if it were a badge of honor. There are many who then become activists and join political efforts to demand "gay rights," denigrate traditional values, and challenge religious freedom. They may do this at least in part to justify their bad sexual behaviors. In reality, those who claim an identity based on arbitrary sexual orientations and bad behaviors have no basis for any special rights or privileges. They are already protected by the same laws as everyone else according to our Constitution.

No one is born gay.

Whether such feelings come uninvited or are willfully chosen, they are still dangerous and outside God's boundaries. People who insist that they are permanently same-sex attracted or gay, and people who identify themselves as members of the LGBTQ community, have turned their backs on truth, nature, and God. They have chosen a wrong path through this dangerous jungle and a huge stampeding animal is after them, whether they realize it or not.

In this chapter we've discussed several ways in which God-given sexuality is no joke. Like an elephant gone wild, sexuality gone wild hurts people in many ways. In the next chapter you'll learn how to keep your sexuality within God's boundaries by applying basic gospel principles.

9

Savage or Saint?

– *applying the gospel* –

You've probably heard of C. S. Lewis who wrote *The Chronicles of Narnia.* He once said that in the morning when we wake up it may seem as if all our problems and wishes come rushing at us "like wild animals." If we are followers of Christ, our first job of the day is to push those worries and wants back and remember who we are, why we are here, and where we want to end up. In other words, focus on spiritual things instead. C. S. Lewis says to let "that larger, stronger, quieter life come flowing in." He reminds us to keep doing this all through the day. We can live that kind of life by applying the most basic parts of the gospel. This is what can make us Latter-day Saints instead of latter-day savages.

In the last chapter we talked about some of the ways people abuse their sexuality. We compared these abuses to being chased by a dangerous wild elephant. By applying the gospel of Jesus Christ we can avoid these dangers altogether or change directions quickly if we are going the wrong way, and grow spiritually at the same time.

Nobody's Perfect . . .

The first gospel concept to discuss here is the concept of sin. Sin is an unpopular word today. Many people don't like the idea of a clear right and wrong, such as God's law of chastity. They don't want to worry about God judging them. But sin is very real. In fact, Nephi explains that if there were no sin, no laws, and no punishments, there would be no God and no righteousness, and we would all vanish away (2 Nephi 2:13).

Compared to God, we all have a long way to go.

You need to know that no human being is perfect. Some may have good intentions, some may have acquired some wisdom, some may shine at certain times, some may be highly esteemed by many people. Some, such as prophets and apostles, are set apart as special witnesses of Christ. But compared to God, no human being is perfectly good or pure or wise or brave or strong.

All of us fall short, even when we don't realize it. We are careless or thoughtless. We miss opportunities to help others. We think we are helping when we are really hurting. We think wrong thoughts. We do good things but for selfish reasons. We lack faith and give in to discouragement. We fall to temptations, big or small, in our thoughts or actions. We forget God. We get puffed up in our pride. We make the wrong choices. We might even willfully and rebelliously disobey God's laws. Then, whatever wrong we do, we tend to excuse ourselves and compare ourselves to others, and decide we haven't done anything *too* wrong.

Well, all of the above, and many more, are sins. Because the word sin has become unpopular, some people like to call them weaknesses, shortcomings, faults, failings, or imperfections. But it doesn't matter what we call them. They show that we are human and have a long way to go.

If we're concerned about the celestial kingdom (eternal life, the kind of life God wants to give us), then it doesn't really matter if our sins are large or small. What matters is that they disqualify us to be in the presence of Heavenly Father. We can't go where He is in our sinful state. Even if we have the best of intentions, even if we do our best to make amends for our errors, even if we love and serve God and our fellow men, even if we work doubly hard to make up for the bad we've done, we still fall short. It is not in our power to erase any of the wrongs we've felt or thought or said or done.

Order in the Court!

Here on Earth our society has established civil laws to keep it safe and orderly. When these laws are broken, our courts weigh all the evidence and circumstances and have the responsibility to affix the proper punishment to a crime. This is what we call justice. Sometimes a punishment is tempered by mercy. For instance, a judge might reduce a sentence if a criminal is a first-time offender, is remorseful, or shows good behavior.

We are also subject to an eternal or divine type of justice. Eternal justice is not forgiving like human justice may be. The heavenly file folder containing our faults is going to condemn us when we are judged by God no matter how hard we've tried to be good. And because we are imperfect human beings, we are not capable of rescuing ourselves from eternal or divine punishment. We are left empty-handed, helpless, in the face of our sins.

We are not able to rescue ourselves.

We'll use Earth's gravity again for a simple example. Say Tarzan decides to leave his lonely jungle life and he's being flown to civilization in an airplane. He looks out the window at the only home he's ever known and gets really homesick. Suddenly he wishes he could go back. Now, he hasn't had any formal education, but he's had enough experience swinging among the treetops, and probably slipping and falling a time or two, to know that if he jumped out of the plane he wouldn't survive.

The principle of Earth's gravity is true and unforgiving. If you jumped out of a plane without a parachute, you'd fall to the earth and this experience would end your life. The same is true for sin and punishment. Here on Earth all accountable people are in a fallen state. We sin to some degree whether we mean to or not. Once we break one of God's laws, we are subject to the consequences of breaking it, like falling to the ground without a parachute, unless someone else pays the price of justice. Someone perfect.

Christ Paid the Price

Because Heavenly Father knows all about these everlasting principles—law, sin, punishment, and justice—He knew we would need mercy. This is why He sent His Son to be our Savior, our Rescuer, our Deliverer, our Redeemer. For this merciful saving grace, or Atonement, to work it would have to be done voluntarily by a perfect and unselfish Being. It would have to be the particular kind of sacrifice that would satisfy eternal justice. Jesus Christ is that Savior. He paid that price for every human being. It's a little like being miraculously saved from the consequences of falling

Jesus accomplished the Atonement out of love for Heavenly Father and His children.

to the earth without a parachute. What's more, Jesus died for us without any thought of reward. He died for all of God's children even knowing most of them would choose to reject his priceless gift. Reward and glory were not his motivators. He had higher, purer reasons. He accomplished the Atonement because he loves Heavenly Father and he loves us perfectly. He wanted to make possible the Father's glorious plan for us.

The Book of Mormon tells of talented speakers called Anti-Christs who became very popular. They tried all kinds of ways to shake the people's faith in Heavenly Father and Jesus. One way they did this was by teaching that there is no such thing as sin and no need for a Savior. We know this isn't so. As Christians we place our faith and hope in Jesus as the only way to gain eternal life.

We have Anti-Christs today, too. These are outspoken people who reject Christ and attract followers. Some deny the very existence of God. By so doing they feel they can break His commandments, including the law of chastity, without fear of eternal punishment. When negative consequences occur here on earth, such as sexually transmitted diseases, they deny responsibility, pass the blame, and expect others to heal them with modern medicines. They react angrily when people take a stand against their bad ideas and behaviors.

Anti-Christs say there is no sin and no need for repentance.

As members of The Church of Jesus Christ, we must center our lives around the Lord and his gospel. The word gospel is the Greek word for good news. Getting saved from that inevitable fall to the earth without a parachute is good news definitely worth knowing about.

Now, we've said that we all sin and that the Savior died for us to pay the price of justice. But what is our part? What must we do for this amazing redemption which qualifies us for eternal life in the celestial kingdom? The 4th Article of Faith answers this question: "We believe that the first principles and ordinances of the Gospel are: first, Faith in the Lord Jesus Christ; second, Repentance; third, Baptism by immersion for the remission of sins; fourth, Laying on of hands for the gift of the Holy Ghost." After being baptized, we must continue to have faith, to repent, and to enjoy the gift of the Holy Ghost.

Faith is an Exercise

A young girl got a ten-speed bike one Christmas morning. She had never ridden a bike before. That very day she lugged the shiny new bicycle straight outside to the street in front of her house. She got on the bike and promptly crashed against the curb. Surprised, the girl pulled herself and her new bike up off the ground, wincing from a bloody scrape on her leg. She really wanted to learn to ride the bike and remembered her parents saying that the bike would stay upright if she kept peddling. At first she didn't believe this, but began to see that the bike balanced itself longer and longer with each try. After that first day, riding a bike seemed to come naturally. She loved riding up and down the hills of a shady park near her house. She continued to love bike riding all her life. Exercising faith is like hopping on a bicycle for the first time. We just have to start pedaling.

Faith is like hopping on a bike for the first time.

What should we have faith in? We can answer this question with the 1st Article of Faith. "We believe in God the Eternal

Father, in His Son Jesus Christ, and in the Holy Ghost." Notice that the kind of faith we are talking about is spiritual. It's not about relying on anything here on earth, ourselves, or other human beings. It's about getting our good feelings of self worth from Heavenly Father. It's about getting our strength and hope from Jesus Christ who offers us redemption and eternal life. It's about getting our instructions from the Holy Ghost.

It is up to each of us to exercise faith that the world is set up just this way for one great and grand purpose: so we can be prepared for the gift of eternal life by way of Christ. Of course each of us chooses whether or not to use this mortal experience for what it is intended. If we want to we can choose the carnal or natural man way. This view is very popular in today's jungle of bad ideas. It focuses on everything happening here on earth as if this is all there is, as if there is no God and no judgment and no heaven. Or we can choose the holy or spiritual way, working to overcome our natural selves by humbly relying on Christ's Atonement. This is the Christ-centered view. It focuses on everything happening here on earth—even the disappointments, the difficulties, and the sadness—as part of God's glorious plan to make us more like Him.

Many people get bogged down by the suffering and injustice of this world. They want to blame God, or have forgotten that He is the source of understanding and power far beyond their own. It is easy to fall into this trap because we have tender feelings and hate to see what looks to us like meaningless sorrow, struggle, suffering, and injustice. But if we are true followers of Christ we should not let our anxiousness about people and events upset our faith in God and His Plan. We are only human and have limited understanding.

Faith covers everything.

People who forget God may begin to hope and imagine that human beings can fix everything here on earth, from global poverty to world peace to climate changes. Not only is it impossible to fix everything, but the scriptures teach us that man's efforts are nothing compared to the power of God. We should turn to God for help in dealing with these problems.

Repentance is a Gift

Did you know the word repentance, or forms of it, occurs in the Standard Works over 300 times? The gospel of Jesus Christ is a gospel of repentance. The Lord can't save us from our sins and exalt us unless we repent. Repentance is not so much a punishment or series of steps as it is a change of direction, or change of heart. The word repentance means to turn back to God. It is a beautiful blessing we should use every day because here on earth it's very easy to get distracted. Even good things can cause us to forget God. A person who continually turns back to God becomes a truly spiritual, or holy, person. He knows Heavenly Father loves him. He relies on Christ. He feels the Spirit often. He wants to keep the commandments. He seeks to be taught by the Holy Ghost. He is grateful for all his experiences. He learns about holiness. Did you know the phrase *Holiness to the Lord* is inscribed on the outside of all of our temples?

> **We can't return to God unless we repent.**

Of course repentance works for what we think of as serious sins also. If a person commits the kind of sin that requires confession to his bishop, there may be a some temporary consequences that include Church discipline. This discipline is intended to help the person turn back to God rather than as a punishment.

If his heart is changed and he has no more desire to commit the sin, and if a substantial period of time passes without transgression, he can be confident in the Lord that he is clean and forgiven.

Because of Christ's Atonement we have an open invitation to humbly turn back to him at any time for truth, for instruction, and for forgiveness of sins. This includes everything we do wrong, for example, thinking or saying something unkind about someone, caring too much about being popular, or ignoring your mom when she tells you to clean your room. It's best to practice repentance every day. That way, you'll get to know the Lord. You'll have an ongoing relationship with him which will help keep you safe from serious sin. It's simple. You do it through prayer.

It's exciting that everything we experience here on earth has a gospel application, including the strong sexual appetite. It's all part of Heavenly Father's plan. He knows all about it. And you might say that sexual feelings get our attention like nothing else. With that in mind, consider this idea. Our sexual desires can be used to help us grow spiritually. As often as they cause us concern, they can remind us to turn back to God. Sexual feelings can act like a rock under your pillow reminding you to pray about your relationship to the Godhead.

Prayer is a Tool

Repenting, or turning back to God, can be done any time through prayer. It can become a regular and wonderful personal habit. It's good to kneel down, bow your head, close your eyes, fold your arms, and speak out loud to Heavenly Father. But there are many times and places for the kind of prayer that must be in your mind and heart. Prayer can be spoken, thought, or felt. A funny old poem by Sam Walter Foss reveals something important about sincere prayer.

The Prayer of Cyrus Brown

"The proper way for a man to pray,"
Said Deacon Lemuel Keyes,
"And the only proper attitude
Is down upon his knees."

"No, I should say the way to pray,"
Said Reverend Doctor Wise,
"Is standing straight with outstretched arms
And rapt and upturned eyes."

"Oh, no, no, no," said Elder Slow,
"Such posture is too proud.
A man should pray with eyes fast-closed
And head contritely bowed."

"It seems to me his hands should be
Austerely clasped in front
With both thumbs pointing toward the ground,"
Said Reverend Doctor Blunt.

"Last year I fell in Hidgekin's well
Headfirst," said Cyrus Brown,
"With both my heels a-stickin' up
And my head a-pointin' down."

"And I made a prayer right then and there,
The best prayer I ever said,
The prayingest prayer I ever prayed,
A-standin' on my head."

It's doubtful we'll ever find ourselves falling down a well. But in many situations we'll feel just as desperate and helpless as Cyrus Brown. It may well be in spiritual rather than physical ways. How are we going to get spiritual help in a crisis, large or small, if we aren't used to drawing out our hearts in prayer?

When we pray we communicate with Heavenly Father in the name of Christ, or by way of Christ. That means Jesus is listening and makes this communication with the Father possible. In our prayers we should be mindful that Jesus is our mediator.

The scriptures say to "pray always." Always is a pretty tall order. It doesn't seem possible. But we can all improve. We can pray on our knees regularly and in our thoughts throughout the day. Sometimes our prayers will be long, and sometimes they'll be short. We can work toward having our hearts and minds turned toward Heavenly Father, Jesus, and the Holy Ghost more often. We can pray when we're thankful for something, when we need something, when we especially need the Spirit, to get spiritually focused in the middle of a busy day, when we're confused or troubled, and when we realize we've thought or done something the least bit weak or wrong. Whenever or however we pray, our prayers can be "the prayingest prayers" we ever said.

Prayer can be spoken, thought, or felt.

Isn't it nice to know that you can never pray too much or too often? For instance, if you want to you can continue to pray after you've closed a formal prayer. There's no rule that says once we get up off our knees or unfold our arms or open our eyes our communication with God has to stop. We can pray as we wake up, pray as we go about our day, pray as we fall asleep.

Cyrus Brown didn't have much time to pray when he was falling down the well, but we usually have plenty of time for talking to Heavenly Father. It's best not to spend too much of that time praying about your troubles, shortcomings, or sins. Heavenly Father knows all about those and dwelling on them doesn't help. How about spending most of your prayer time talking about God and your relationship to Him? You can pray about who Heavenly Father and Jesus are, how much They love you, who you are, why you're here on earth (to gain a body and exercise faith in Christ toward eternal life), your reliance on Christ and the Holy Ghost, your gratitude to Heavenly Father, and many other spiritual truths. How about praying to grow spiritually and to know God's will for you? When we pray like this we are turning back to God as Jesus invites us to do. This is how we can really get to know the Lord.

You can pray anytime.

It's easy to forget to pray often because of all the distractions around us. Most people need some sort of reminder. For example, you could get into the habit of sending up a little prayer—just a few words—whenever you do something that recurs throughout the day, such as when you walk in or out of your bedroom, whenever you hang up the phone, whenever you go to your locker, or whenever you wash your face or change your clothes. Think of some way to remind yourself to turn back to God throughout the day to talk to Him about those basics.

It might be very helpful to write down things to pray about, perhaps in your journal, and read this often until you get used to praying about spiritual truths. Such a prayer can have the following elements in it. (It's nice to use some formal prayer language as we have here, but if it trips you up, just speak naturally):

Heavenly Father, I know Thou art my Father. I know I have a Heavenly Mother, too. I know I am Thy spirit son (or daughter) and that I am loved perfectly by Thee. Thou lovest me and all Thy children more than I can imagine. I know I have great worth. I understand that my value has nothing to do with what I look like, what I think, feel, or do, or how others treat me. Because of Thy love I will value myself and treat myself with great respect. When I feel Thy love for me I love and respect others more. It's so important to me to know who I am. I thank Thee for this knowledge.

I also know why I am here and where I am going. I came to earth for two reasons: to get a body and to choose to live with Thee again. This is only possible because of Jesus Christ. I'm so grateful for my Savior. I know Jesus loves me. I know I need him. He's the only way for me to make it back to Thee. Help me to remember I have a lot to learn. I know it's because of Jesus that I can keep learning and growing spiritually. I know this is Thy will for me so I can be prepared for eternal life in the celestial kingdom.

I love Thee, Heavenly Father. I love the Lord Jesus Christ. Help me to love Thee more and more. Please send the Spirit of the Lord, the Holy Ghost, to be with me always, to remind me of all that is true, to correct me, and to guide me in my feelings, thoughts, and actions. Help me to feel Thy great love for me now and all the time. Help me to be steadfast in Christ. Help me to listen to the still, small voice . . .

You can start praying like this right away. The exact words you use are not important, but praying about these truths is. If you pray humbly like this throughout the day, and really mean it, great things will start to happen in your spiritual life.

The Holy Ghost is the Best Teacher

When you were confirmed a member of the Church, you were given the gift of the Holy Ghost. The Holy Ghost is also called the Spirit of the Lord. He is the voice of the Lord Jesus Christ that reaches us personally and lets us know for ourselves the truth of all things (Moroni 10:5). This is personal revelation. The real thing. The best way to be open to the Holy Ghost is through prayer. For example, if you pray often about spiritual truths such as those mentioned above, you invite the Holy Ghost to be with you. Pretty soon the Holy Ghost will confirm to you that what you are praying about is true. Peace and joy will come to you from this spiritual source.

Having the Spirit with you is what it means to be a spiritual person. This presence is very sacred. Often referred to as the still, small voice, the Holy Ghost teaches, comforts, warns, and strengthens. It is a gift Jesus said we must ask for as if knocking on a door. We are most influenced by the Spirit when our fondest wish is to do Heavenly Father's will with our reliance on Christ.

All good thoughts, feelings, ideas, discoveries, and solutions come through the Holy Ghost. If we have the Spirit with us we are full of courage, faith, and gratitude to God. We are eager to learn. We pray to know how to grow spiritually, improve ourselves, and best serve others. We find great meaning and purpose in all our activities and go about our daily tasks filled with the love of God and everyone we see.

The Holy Ghost will confirm truth.

During the sacrament we pray to always have the Lord's Spirit with us. The Holy Ghost can be your constant companion. In this jungle of falsehoods we live in today, you will especially need him. You need to see clearly what is truly good and what is truly evil. A good habit to get into is to filter everything you think and hear past the Holy Ghost. If you seek to be taught by him, he will teach you everything you should do (2 Nephi 32:5). You'll have a sense of peace and know in your heart and mind what is right.

We have talked about sin, justice, the Savior, faith, repentance, prayer, and the Holy Ghost. You might call learning about and applying these gospel basics *spiritual good works*. We tend to think of good works as performances like going to church, paying tithing, serving a mission, fulfilling Church callings, and doing service. We forget that spiritual good works are commandments, too.

Can't we just do good things and not worry so much about all this spiritual stuff? Sure we can, if that's what we want. There are many, many kind and generous people who do lots of good things, but who give no thought to God. They may even be atheists and not believe in God at all. Much more is required of a Latter-day Saint. The Lord warns us about not doing our spiritual homework. He says to love God with all our heart, soul, mind, and strength (Mark 12:30). He asks us how we can possibly know a master we have not served (Mosiah 5:13)? He says that if we do not do

Good works are spiritual too.

When we put first things first, we'll do more good than we thought possible.

Heavenly Father's will we do not know Christ and will be invited to depart from his presence (JST, Matthew 7:23). People who don't keep striving to put God first in their hearts do not have the celestial kingdom as their goal.

Alma in The Book of Mormon said that if we do our inner spiritual work, good outward works will follow (Alma 7:24). When we put first things first, we'll probably do more good works than we thought possible. And we'll be doing them for the right reasons, the exalting reasons. As an added bonus, if we do our spiritual homework we will feel the Spirit more, be happier, treat others better, and want to make right choices all the time.

What about enduring to the end? Enduring to the end is a common phrase in the Church. Another way to say this is being steadfast in Christ (2 Nephi 31:20). But what does being steadfast in Christ really mean? Another word for steadfast is faithful, meaning full of faith. When we are steadfast it means that no matter what the world around us is saying, and no matter how we fall short, we believe Christ is our Savior. When we totally and sincerely trust in Christ we become so grateful that we start to be better people. We not only begin to overcome our sins, we begin to develop God-like attributes. With those attributes we'll feel at home in God's presence and want to continue in our progression. And this is what life with God, or eternal life, is all about.

You can practice being faithful, or steadfast in Christ, every day. Whenever you happen to catch some of the world's wrong ideas about Christ, about sexuality, or about anything, you can hop on your spiritual bicycle, start pedaling, and do your best with a prayer in your heart. Whenever you get feeling bored, lonely, embarrassed, inadequate, unsatisfied, prideful, sad, selfish, weak, afraid, discouraged, ashamed, or guilty, you now know how to make the needed changes. You can pray about Heavenly Father and Jesus and Their relationship to you. Through the Holy Ghost you will feel loved and know what needs correcting inside and out. The gospel of Jesus Christ enables us to start again, as many times as it takes, and move forward.

Remember, the only way Heavenly Father can shape us up for eternity is to let us loose in this jungle we call earth life, with the gospel as our map to show us the way back home. It's not supposed to be easy. For instance, life would be much simpler if boys and girls, men and women, did not have to deal with sexuality. The stampeding sexuality occurring today can trick and trap us. But sexuality also gives us opportunities to sort out feelings and decide that sexual activity outside of marriage is wrong and sinful. The gospel truth about sexuality prompts us to be interested in marriage and children. A desire to handle our sexual feelings properly reminds us to turn back to God often. Without such choices we would be more like robots, without feelings, without free will, and without the ability to progress.

The only way Heavenly Father can shape us up is to let us loose.

We chose to come here to learn what we could not learn in our premortal life. But we need to do our spiritual homework. We can begin this now, today, and feel prepared to meet God at any time. Through our tiny daily decisions each of us indicates which we want to be: a savage or a saint.

10
Out on a Limb
– chastity and serving a mission –

What about sexuality and serving a mission? A full-time mission is like Tarzan being out on a limb for two whole years, safe above the elephant stampede. Or is it? This chapter is addressed mainly to boys because serving a mission is primarily a young man's priesthood responsibility and because sexuality can be a troublesome issue especially for boys before, during, or after the mission. But the same principles apply to girls as well.

First let's think about missions in general. Latter-day prophets have taught that every young man should look forward to serving a mission. In the LDS culture a mission has become something like becoming a high school football star. A boy dreams about it all his life, finally gets to try out, qualifies, and gets picked. He joins the group, is instructed by coaches, and endures intensive training. He immerses himself in everyday practices and plays big games that are sometimes won and sometimes lost. He enjoys some degree of attention, excitement, status, and congratulations, and then remembers the unique experience as the high point of his life. Whew! It's a great time. But when it comes to serving a mission, there is something wrong with this picture. If a young man's mission turns out to be the spiritual high point of his life, gravity will take him downhill from there.

The gospel basics we talked about in the previous chapter are for always. You should be doing your spiritual homework now, during your mission, and all through your life. The best preparation for serving a mission is to understand and apply the principles of faith and repentance, to get into the habit of sincere prayer, and feeling the influence of the Spirit. If you begin early developing your relationship with Heavenly Father, Jesus Christ, and the Holy Ghost, you'll not only be progressing along every day but will surely want to go on a full-time mission in the future to spread the good news. In this way, you are growing closer to the Lord now and will be a better missionary later because of it.

To prepare for a mission, do your spiritual homework now.

Let's define some of the words associated with missions and missionaries: righteousness, worthiness, and sexual purity. These are words we hear so often we may not realize, or we may forget, what they really mean and that we should be striving toward them always.

Righteousness means rightness, goodness, everything that God is. It's a character trait, not a list of accomplishments. We can't be perfectly righteous, as God is, but we can desire righteousness and wholeheartedly work toward it from the inside out.

Worthiness, or being worthy, in this sense has nothing to do with your great worth as a human being and child of God. We use the word worthy to determine the requirements for a temple recommend and a mission.

Righteousness is a character trait, not a list of accomplishments.

But those outward requirements, such as church attendance, paying tithing, and abstaining from sexual activity outside of marriage, may not indicate true worthiness. True worthiness is indicated by your heart, what you care about, what you think about, and what your motivations are.

Sexual purity, like righteousness and worthiness, concerns our hearts, minds, and actions. Remember, thoughts can be chaste or unchaste and lead to corresponding feelings and actions. Any boy of any age who is experiencing sexual confusion, addiction, or transgression, needs to start taking care of these problems now. If they are not resolved, these problems can hinder his spiritual progress, lead to more or worse problems, and get in the way of serving a mission later on. Wrong ideas and behaviors should be confessed and forsaken. Some sexual issues may be symptoms of deeper problems and misconceptions that can be rooted out and corrected with family, religious, and professional help. Any healthy person can be free of sexual sin by turning back to God through sincere repentance and application of the Atonement of Jesus Christ.

Hold the same truths in your mind now as when you're serving a mission.

We've talked about righteousness, worthiness, and sexual purity. Now is the time to work on these attributes. You now know that the kind of person you really are—your actual personal righteousness, worthiness, and sexual purity—is invisible to everyone but you and the Lord. Because of agency, the kind of person you are outside *and inside* is totally up to you.

What about when a young man is finally on a mission? He leaves his family, friends, job, school, interests, and ambitions behind. He makes a sacrifice, he takes the risks, he goes out on a limb. He must obey God's law of chastity, and put off dating, too. In other words, for Tarzan a mission amounts to two years with no Jane. All dating and plans for marriage are temporarily set aside. As always, he must also keep his thoughts, feelings, attitudes, and language chaste.

To keep sexuality on hold and in its proper context (marriage), young men can review the following truths as often as needed, on the mission or any time:

1. Young men have frequent and involuntary erections. It's part of physical development. Don't overanalyze it or panic because of it. It's just simple biology.

2. There are a few annoying, inconvenient, and potentially embarrassing things about being a male, just as there are for being a female. Treat your body with respect and consider any sexual feelings a reminder that you have exactly what it will take to be a loving husband and father. Redirect your thoughts to gratitude to Heavenly Father and reliance on Christ. The Holy Ghost will prompt you toward wholesome thoughts and activities.

3. As a missionary you will have several companions and probably make strong lifelong friendships. Admiring someone of your same sex is perfectly

natural. It's wonderful to be a male, be with other males, and belong to the Male Club of the World. But in this oversexualized world, some young men may need to be reminded not to sexualize their need for belonging and close friendships.

4. Remember that it's healthy and right to set aside sexual feelings until marriage.

5. Enjoy looking forward to getting married at the right time to the right person in the right place. One of the reasons young men should want to get married is so they can channel all their sexual energy into the only productive and correct direction.

A mission is a unique and wonderful time. Intense prayer and concentrated scripture study, plus the structure, support, and close companionships, make these two years very memorable. Relationships with companions and mission presidents take shape that may last forever. Sometimes eternal spiritual bonds are forged between missionaries and converts. But remember, these years should not turn out to be the best two years of anyone's life. Spiritually speaking, we should have exciting religious adventures before a mission and many, many increasingly wonderful adventures after it, so many we quickly lose count. Think of it this way: If a young man lives to be 100, a mission is only two percent of his lifetime. Surely he wouldn't want to miss out on spiritual growth for the other 98 percent!

So what is a potential missionary's first responsibility? It is to work out his own salvation by applying in his everyday life the basic principles of the gospel we talked about in chapter nine such as faith, repentance, and the Holy Ghost. He'll be a lot better missionary if he has developed his personal relationship with Jesus Christ well before he slips on that name tag. That's what we call raising the bar—or limb.

11

A Treehouse of Your Own

– proper sexuality in marriage –

Is a snug tree house the safest place in the jungle for a grown-up Tarzan to bring his new wife Jane, or is this just a romantic notion? Sure, a tree house would sit safely above any stampeding elephants, but what about all the openings that could admit other dangers? Stealthy leopards and slithering pythons can climb trees.

Marriage is not the end of being chaste, not by any means. Remember, we are commanded to be chaste all our lives. Contrary to some wrong ideas we hear in our modern-day jungle, a married man and woman still have boundaries set by God for sexual thoughts, feelings, and conduct. Chastity, or sexual purity, is a lifelong obligation, in marriage as well as outside of marriage. In respectful marriage between a man and a woman the sexual appetite has a wholesome, manageable, and meaningful outlet. Sexual desires are safely and productively channeled. Anything outside these boundaries is unchaste and will have tragic consequences.

> **Chastity is a lifelong obligation, in or out of marriage.**

TREE
SWEET
TREE

We know that sexual impurity begins quietly in a person's mind. In marriage, impure thoughts can quickly poison the marriage relationship. Evidently, sexuality can stampede dangerously out of control in any stage or situation of life. In this chapter we'll talk about how you can prepare for a healthy, wholesome, enjoyable tree house of your own. We'll review how applying gospel principles is the best defense against stealthy, slithering, out-of-place sexuality, even within marriage.

Why do people get married? What purposes does marriage serve? Just decades ago the answers to these questions were so obvious that no one felt the need to ask them. Now, the very idea of marriage is being challenged. Questions like these are being asked so often and answered so incorrectly that the whos, whys, and whats of marriage have been blurred. Suddenly we need to understand the important reasons for marriage or we risk falling right out of the ideal marriage tree house.

There are good reasons for marriage between a man and a woman.

Let's start with perhaps the most basic moral value that exists among the human family. It is that we should care deeply about our posterity (children), about welcoming them, about loving them, and about teaching them. A man and a woman are the only human unit capable of reproducing. Ideally, a sacred marriage commitment is made between a husband and wife which grows stronger with time and experience, providing security and safety for each family member. Knowing this, human societies throughout time have gone out of their way to institute, legitimize, and support marriage between a man and a woman through public policies and laws. This support fits in perfectly with God's laws, biology, human needs and desires, and the best interests of children.

Within marriage, ideally, the woman makes a home while the man protects and provides for the family. The solemn marriage covenant is an unspoken guarantee that the children who come from this couple will be provided for and nurtured. The man limits his sexual desires to his wife alone so that all the children he fathers may thrive in a secure family. The wife promises to be faithful also so that her husband can know these children are indeed his. It comes down to a trust between the man and the woman, a trust that is supported by society and God. This is why people make a marriage ceremony a special event like no other. It's a celebration! A marriage between a man and a woman is great cause for everyone to rejoice.

> **Human beings should care about their posterity.**

Traditional marriage is the foundation not only of strong families but of a strong society. Adults are healthier and happier when united and committed in traditional marriage. Children do better in every way when they are raised by a married mother and father. In marriage, people make promises and vow publicly to keep them. These promises require hard work and come with awesome responsibilities. A husband and wife who keep their promises and fulfill their responsibilities to each other are teaching their children how to be honest and productive citizens.

> **Marriage is a celebration.**

But marriage is much more than a way to ensure that families and society run smoothly here on earth. Besides all the practical reasons for traditional marriage, marriage also has a lot to do with making us better people. Marriage gives us many opportunities to grow spiritually. As Latter-day Saints we believe marriage helps prepare us to live with Heavenly Father in the celestial kingdom.

Young people usually have a romantic idea about marriage that may not be completely accurate. It's true that marriage can be very wonderful. But you need to know that marriage is much more than romance, and much more than sex. Some experts say that the physical part is only a small percent of the marriage relationship. It might feel like a bigger part at first, but marriage soon gets down to all the many facets of life and living with all the inevitable ups and downs. There may even come some difficulties that rock the tree house at its foundations. Marriages must weather those storms. That's why we make promises of love, fidelity, and devotion from the very first. Married people have made a promise that they'll devote themselves to this one particular person of the opposite sex through thick and thin. They are supposed to do things for each other and with each other, thus fulfilling certain expectations.

Marriage makes us better people.

This isn't always easy. In fact, it would sometimes probably be much easier to live with someone of the same sex, like a friend or roommate, than a spouse. People of the same sex have some very basic things in common. They may experience less difficulties in their relationship than if they were opposite sexes. Some are saying it is good for two men or two women to be married to each other. Gay or same-sex marriage is a huge issue in

Marriage is only between a man and a woman.

our society today. But this is not marriage. Marriage, by definition, can only occur between opposite sexes. Not only is the idea of same-sex marriage absurd, but sexual behavior between same sexes is sinful, unnatural, harmful, and contrary to God's law of chastity and His plan for us.

You need to know that marriage will not automatically make a person chaste. Anyone involved in sexual sin of any kind should resolve the problem, temptation, or transgression before marriage. Otherwise, sexual impurity could worsen or take new paths that will cause trauma and suffering to many others besides oneself.

Before marriage, every Tarzan and Jane should talk about and agree on proper attitudes about sexual behavior. They should see each other as a whole person, a living, striving soul, never as an object to be used only for selfish pleasure. In other words, Tarzan should primarily be thinking of Jane, not sex. And the same goes for Jane. If a married couple is most concerned about each other's overall happiness, sexual relations will be more enjoyable.

Sexual intimacy is only intimate when it is private.

You should know that real sexual intimacy in marriage is very private and personal. Unfortunately, much of society has presumed to make the act of sexual intimacy public, treating sex in a very casual, impersonal way. What is often shown in art, in advertising, on TV, in movies, in romance novels, and always in pornography, is playacting with no meaningful relationships and no responsibilities attached. Only in proper marriage is the sexual act meaningful. What you should plan for is the real thing. It's worth waiting for, and worth protecting by keeping private. That is what civilized, well-mannered people do.

Marriage is an act of faith. It is an institution based on faith in God who ordained it and faith in one's self and one's spouse to keep promises. In a healthy, respectful marriage, the husband and wife care very much about the wholesome needs and desires of each other, sexually and in every other way. President Hinckley said that love in marriage will "flourish and blossom . . . if there is an anxious looking-after the happiness of one's companion."

Of course no marriage is perfect, even under the most ideal circumstances. That's because no human being is perfect. It's another very good reason that we need a Savior. Developing one's personal relationship with Christ, as we talked about in chapter nine, will expand, enrich, and secure a marriage. This includes being chaste, meaning keeping sexual thoughts and desires within God's boundaries.

Personal relationships with Christ can expand, enrich, and secure a marriage.

Especially today, married couples need to help each other be chaste and faithful. Wives and husbands must be sensitive to the very real temptations in our permissive environment. Each person needs to know that the other is not necessarily immune to these temptations. When both husband and wife continually turn back to Christ, a marriage will be safeguarded against all forms of unchastity in thought and deed.

The world around us pushes many false ideas about marriage, including that it's too difficult, that it need not or cannot be permanent, that it is possible between same sexes, and that it doesn't have to include fidelity and chastity. Have you noticed how many Hollywood stars' real-life marriages seem to come and go like box-office hits? Some radio and TV shows portray pornography as helpful to sexual intimacy in marriage. A recent *Oprah* TV program even presumed to show adultery as helpful to marriage. All these ideas fall outside God's law of chastity. We need to continually reject these worldly views with the help of the Spirit.

For Latter-day Saints a successful marriage is made up of the following:

> 1. Two adults of the opposite sex who are compatible and attracted to each other physically, socially, spiritually, and intellectually.
>
> 2. A shared commitment to the gospel of Jesus Christ which includes everything true and right and good.

These are the foundational materials they'll need to build a safe and cozy tree house of their very own.

12

The One Right Path

– following Christ alone –

Speaking of jungles, a young girl and her family once moved from California to an island in the Pacific Ocean. A thick, dark jungle grew behind their house. In it grew tangan-tangan trees, pago trees, mango trees, pai pai trees, palm trees, and fan-dan trees. There was bermudagrass, sawgrass, African tulips, bamboo, and hibiscus. The locals call this wild forest the boonies. The boonies grow and grow. Every now and then the girl's dad would get out his machete (a long, wide-blade knife) and hack away at the fast-growing bushes and trees to keep them from encroaching on the house. It was hard work and he immediately became drenched in sweat in the humid tropical climate.

One day, this young girl was convinced by some neighborhood boys to go boonie stomping with them, meaning hiking through the pathless boonies. She liked to hike and thought it sounded fun. The boys didn't tell her of the dangers. They actually wanted to scare her a little so they could feel important. It worked. She got stuck in a muddy cave, stung by mosquitoes, and became disoriented. She had to rely completely on those

mischievous boys and their machetes to get her out of that thick jungle. It was an adventure she never repeated.

Imagine trying to make your way through something like the boonies back to Heavenly Father. What if you couldn't find the one right path? What if all you could see was a thick stubborn wall of jungle? What if those you depended on cared more about themselves than you? You could get tangled and trapped.

Our world today is like the boonies, that jungle of lies about God and sexual morality. It has encroached on our culture, our freedoms, our way of life, and our progress. Those boonies continue to grow perhaps faster than they can be cut down. The scriptures say that to survive spiritually we need to use not our own strength or willpower, not the philosophies of men, but the word of God which is more powerful on our minds than any other thing, more powerful even than a sword (Alma 31:5). We've been talking about the word of God, or the gospel of Jesus Christ, throughout this book. It is like a spiritual sword or machete that will clear our path back to Heavenly Father.

The gospel is powerful.

American culture has not always been tangled up in sexual immorality. It's important to know the truth about our special nation's history and how it relates to human sexuality stampeding dangerously out of control today.

In the 1776 Declaration of Independence we learn that the United States of America was founded on the truth that there is a God, a Supreme Being, who cares what happens to us. The Founders of this country proclaimed that this nation would only survive if it were built on a moral and religious foundation. They trusted that Americans would be a moral and religious people.

They took for granted that Americans would realize that freedom comes with responsibilities and some important restraints. They also knew that our noble-minded and idealistic Constitution would become a license for disaster if the people turned away from Christianity, which includes God's law of chastity.

Did you know that America's first school text book was the Bible? For a long time it was the *only* textbook. Children learned the alphabet and how to read using the scriptures alone. For hundreds of years our public schools used lessons from the Bible to teach children how to be good citizens.

Besides the Bible being used as the basis for public education in past centuries, our country's motto, "In God We Trust," is engraved on our coins and printed on our paper money, contained in the lyrics of our national anthem, and inscribed on the walls of countless government buildings. These words are embossed in gold, front and center, in the House of Representatives chamber in Washington D.C. We are "one nation under God" in our Pledge of Allegiance. Many, many monuments and buildings across America have inscriptions that refer to God directly. Every day in our courts people swear to tell the truth by placing a hand on the Bible.

God is the foundation of America.

And yet, in spite of America's rich Christian heritage and the advancements it has made because of its foundation on Christianity (such as abolishing slavery and giving women the right to vote), the past century witnessed America gradually rejecting God and His laws. Just from what we've related so far about American history, you can see that this movement away from God is actually *un*American. It was in the early 1960s that laws were passed that formally took God out of schools. After hundreds of years, there was to be no more prayer, no more Bible, no more God. Many people born before the 1960s remember participating in formal prayers in school such as blessings on the food. After that, children began to grow up with the idea that anything religious or God-centered was not to be talked about in public school. Actually, there is no legal reason this has to be so. We have just been gradually conditioned into thinking God has no business in our government and public education. It's not hard to imagine what God, who created everything, including us, thinks of that.

Christianity is the foundation of America's heritage and culture. The free practice of religion is the first freedom in the First Amendment, guaranteed by the Constitution. The only check on religion in our Constitution is found in the First Amendment which states that Congress (part of our national government) cannot establish a particular church every American must belong to or support financially. Our nation's founders wanted to make sure we didn't have another Church of England situation where people were forced by the king to financially support a church they didn't attend or believe in. Every American was to be free to worship God according to the dictates of his own conscience.

Our constitution guarantees religious freedom.

Ironically, even though most Americans still profess to believe in God, our mainstream media, public and higher education, and some of our laws and public policies generally no longer reflect that belief. It seems everybody has agreed to confine God to one place and time: church on Sunday, and He's not welcome or proper anywhere else. Perhaps many of us who profess to be religious are too much like the Zoramites in The Book of Mormon whose strange form of worship astonished Alma and his brethren.

One day a week the Zoramites took turns climbing to the top of the Rameumptom or "holy stand" to loudly and enthusiastically proclaim how much they loved God and wanted to serve Him. They talked about how superior they were to unbelievers. Then they went home and never spoke of God, that is, until a week later when they climbed up the Rameumptom again and said the same old automatic, prideful prayer. They were only pretending to be religious (Alma 31).

> **It's easy to become like the Zoramites.**

It's easy to fall into that trap. We might be doing a great job of going through the motions. But we could all use some improvement when it comes to living our religion in our hearts, hour by hour, day by day, seven days a week.

Some people, like the Zoramites, deny God inwardly while others deny him outright. These are publicly-proclaimed atheists, secularists, and humanists. Some call themselves "progressives." They push the prideful notion that mortal man is the ultimate intelligence or power. They refuse to bow down to God and don't want to appear to follow His laws. These are the type of people who are working tirelessly to try to eliminate every reminder of God in our cultural environment. Having removed God from our schools, they now pressure towns and cities with law suits if they don't get rid of historic monuments and plaques displaying the Ten Commandments in their public places. Groups and individuals are trying to take the words, "under God" out of our Pledge of Allegiance. They are working to have the words "In God We Trust" removed from our money. Who knows what they'll think up next!

These people may say they do this because they believe religion doesn't belong in government. But they are denying the fact that America's Founding Fathers counted on the free and sincere practice of religion in order to keep America safe and good. They deny history which proves that Christianity is the best way to keep people free. It's interesting to note that ever since God was taken out of public education, and sex education put in, sexual immorality, along with all its negative consequences, has increased.

Some noisily push the idea that believing in God is old-fashioned and foolish, even hateful and discriminatory. They badmouth and belittle others' religious beliefs. This sounds exactly like the people in the great and spacious building of Lehi's dream who were pointing at and making fun of those who were struggling to stay on the path to God (1 Nephi 8,12). Many people today don't like the idea of being accountable to God or judged by Him for their thoughts and actions. One area in which people especially like to be free of God is the area of sexual behavior. You can see how today's stampeding sexuality is a symptom of a society that has rejected God.

Many people today follow Anti-Christ philosophies. They like hearing that they are doing great and don't need to repent or improve themselves. They would rather rely on what they can touch and see than exercise faith in God. Our culture as a whole is like that. It tends to turn instead to science for instance, even though science is always changing and making new discoveries. And science pretty much leaves God out. Or does it?

Stampeding sexuality is a symptom of rejecting God.

We know that the great majority of Americans believe in God. This in-

Science need not leave out God.

cludes many scientists. These scientists do not see a conflict between their religious beliefs and their lifelong efforts to explain the natural world. Sadly, scientists who believe in God are increasingly discounted in our mainstream culture even though they are brilliant and have much to offer. That's because their ideas do not fit in with today's worldly and often unscientific views.

You could say the world has taken a major turn away from God, scientifically and culturally, in large measure because of Charles Darwin. He wrote about his famous theory of natural selection, the foundation for the theory of evolution, way back in the middle 1800s, and many people continue to accept some form of his ideas to relieve themselves of having to believe in God. (At the same time, they overlook the parts they don't like, such as Darwin's idea that women's brains are less evolved and smaller than men's.) You'd think the scientific community would have progressed a lot in over 150 years. It has in many ways, but not when it comes to Darwin. Darwin's theory is taught in most American schools as if it were a fact. People conveniently forget it was only a theory, a theory that even Darwin himself knew would fall to pieces if new scientific evidence about life was discovered, which it was.

About a hundred years after Darwin's theory became famous, amazing technological advances of a kind Darwin never imagined gave scientists new information about what living things are made of and how cells work. For instance, we now know that microscopic cells are not blobs of jelly as Darwin thought, but have special functions and contain intricate biological machines, and that these machines are what is termed "irreducibly complex." In other words, if you take one part of the machine away it won't work. This, and other important scientific information, points out that living things could not have evolved from simple to complex accidentally and gradually. It shows all living things had to be specifically and completely created by an intelligent designer, whom we know to be God. Scientists, religious or not, are finding it difficult to get others scientists and an indoctrinated public to accept these amazing new scientific discoveries. It seems as though proud people want to deny an Intelligence more powerful than themselves. It looks like Darwinism gives people an excuse to act outside God's boundaries.

There is a lot of talk today about freedom. But unfortunately, when you take God and His laws out of the picture, all freedoms may turn to destruction. It's like the trained elephant gone mad. As our Founders knew, freedoms come with restraints or they become dangerous. For example, if there were no personal, social, and legal restraints on the sexual appetite and the ability to procreate, we know there would be a great many more needless abortions, abandoned babies, deserted spouses and families, broken hearts, crimes, and diseases.

When you take God out of the picture, freedom turns dangerous.

You can and should know for yourself that Heavenly Father is real. That truth can change everything. You don't need man's science or anyone else's testimony. Try looking around at the inexplicable wonder and perfection of God's creations that man is learning more and more about every day: the human body and mind, animal and plant life, the earth, the expanding universe. When your thoughts, prayers, and actions reflect your belief in God, this truth will be confirmed by the Holy Ghost.

Latter-day Saints must pay no attention to those who say that believing in God is weak, simplistic, narrow-minded, bigoted, ignorant, self-righteous, cruel, or anything else negative. Perhaps people who push this view are worried that God is real. Maybe that nagging doubt is what makes them feel guilty and angry. Like Nephi's brothers, Laman and Lemuel, they get mad when they hear the truth and they want to shut up the messenger.

In the words of Brigham Young,

> "Pay no attention to the world. You will see plenty of the world—it will be before you all the time—but . . . [by] the Holy Ghost you will at once see the difference between the wisdom of men and the wisdom of God . . . ."

According to the First Amendment, each of us has the right to practice and express our Christian religious beliefs. Remember that religious freedom is the first freedom mentioned in the Constitution's Bill of Rights, that America's Founding Fathers wanted to make sure this essential freedom was protected, and that they knew that humbly believing in God is good and right. True Christianity has the potential of making each person a better person, and every country a better, more free country. Today we must turn away from dark, uncertain paths that lead to the badmouthing of God and religion, the corruption of language, the rewriting of history, the distorting of healthy human sexuality, and the mocking of chastity and marriage. These are some of the many "strange roads" Nephi warned us about (1 Nephi 8:32).

There is also a lot of talk about how everyone is entitled to express their own opinion. Listening to differing opinions and having an open mind about issues that affect us, such as whether or not school should be year-round, is useful. But having an open mind toward arguments against everlasting truths and biological realities is just plain foolish. C. S. Lewis wrote that there may be a dozen views about important things until you know the one right answer. People are allowed to form their own opinions, but important truths remain the same.

Opinions may or may not be based on truth.

Nothing good can come from ignoring or misrepresenting truth. Nothing good can come of giving a voice to evil and falsehood. Many current opinions about matters of great importance are worthless and even dangerous. They are based on fleeting human-minded trends instead of God's eternal laws proven beneficial to mankind for thousands of years. Only God has all the answers. Only God does not change.

Religion at its best is a very good thing. Most religious people believe there is a life after this one and that we will be rewarded or punished according to God's judgment, which belief encourages people to be good. Ideally, we go to church to discuss the welfare of our souls and help each other become better people, the kind of people who desire to live with God again. We should be doing our best to live our religion in our daily lives and share it with others. We know that Heavenly Father is patient with us. If we are followers of Christ, we are obligated to repent always, forgive as we are forgiven by Heavenly Father through Christ, and listen to the Holy Ghost for guidance.

It's trendy to minimize or reject the value of religion by using the argument that all the talk of rules and sins makes us feel guilty, that it damages self-esteem. The truth is, we all sin and should feel bad about it. Guilt can be a healthy way of reminding us something needs fixing for our own good. It is one way the Holy Ghost can point out ways we need correction. If we are confident in Heavenly Father's perfect love and get our good feelings of self worth from that source, we won't mind humbly going about improving ourselves. In fact, we'll be filled with gratitude.

It is true that sometimes human beings distort religion into something worthless, false, or hurtful. All good things can be turned into bad things. Remember our nice firm yellow banana. Now think of it gone bad, all mushy and brown and unappetizing. People, in and out of churches, who twist religion into something evil have turned a nice banana into a spoiled one. We have to learn to separate God's eternal truths from the human flaws we inevitably come across in our church experiences. We need to work at being truly religious, rather than expecting perfection of human beings or treating church only as a sort of club where we get to be with our friends.

We need to work at being truly religious.

Here is what 14-year-old Anne Frank wrote about religion in her famous diary: "People who have a religion should be glad, for not everyone has the gift of believing in heavenly things . . . . A religion keeps a person on the right path." Anne was right. But there are strange paths we must watch for even if we are happy and active in church. It's easy to stray from that one right path, to get on little bypaths that only *seem* clear and open and harmless.

For instance, it's very easy to begin to worship God's creations rather than God, the Creator. If we only emphasize our relationships with each other, we might neglect our relationship with the Godhead. If we center our thoughts on our positions, callings, missions, temple work, and service, we might forget we need a Savior. We can love one another and serve in the Church, all out of love for God, humbly relying on Christ, and giving hearts full of gratitude to Heavenly Father. That's what being religious really means.

We talk a great deal about following Jesus' example of loving and serving one another. We say he is our elder brother and our friend. But we need to be careful to emphasize that Jesus is the Savior of the world. He is not merely concerned with human relationships or outward performances. He is all about spiritual things, about putting first things first, about making us different kinds of people inside and out, about preparing us to live with Heavenly Father in an exalted state. He knows our relationships and performances will improve if we put God first. His life shows that the will of the Father was his own will.

You now have a better understanding of God's law of chastity. This law is one of many tests to see if we will choose God's way or some other path. It doesn't really matter what that other path is. All wrong paths lead away from God. If we choose a different path than the one that leads to Heavenly Father, we begin to distance ourselves from Him. We cannot get to Heavenly Father if we're on the wrong path, just as we can't get to the top of Mount Timpanogos in Utah if we are on the trail to Pike's Peak in Colorado. To correct this mistake we must retrace our steps and begin again. Striving to keep the law of chastity for all the right reasons is one of many opportunities to check which path we're on.

Sure, you're living in a jungle overgrown with some bad ideas. But you can take up the spiritual machete of truth and continually clear that path to Heavenly Father, relying on His love, eternal truths, and the gospel of Jesus Christ. Everything we experience here in mortality can be worthwhile as we work at becoming real Latter-day Saints. And it's only because of Christ that we can make this progress and enjoy this adventure. All of us need the Savior to safely make our way through this overgrown earthly jungle on the one and only path to eternal life.

Armed with the principles we have discussed in this book, young people will not be caught off-guard by what goes on around them or their own sexual feelings. If young people do find themselves being chased by that elephant, they need not become casualties. Come to think of it, Tarzan had a way of calming even stampeding elephants, just as Jesus Christ can make us into new and better creatures. The gospel truth should make us feel so good we could let loose a resounding Tarzan yell.

There is only one right path to God.

Ahhh–ahahahahahah–ahahahahah!

Notes and References

Introduction for Parents

p. i, The quote about Madonna is from *Saving Childhood* by Michael Medved and Diane Medved, Ph.D., HarperCollins Publishers, Inc., New York, 1998, 23.

p. i, Bill O'Reilly said "Evil is in the house," on The Radio Factor, Dec. 11, 2007.

p. ii, The Boyd K. Packer quote is from "Little Children," *Ensign,* Nov 1986, 16.

p.v, The Boyd K. Packer quote is from "Ye Are the Temple of God," *Ensign,* Nov 2000, 72-74.

Chapter 1: What Elephant?

p. 2, The Articles of Faith are found at the end of The Pearl of Great Price.

p. 3, The law of chastity is found throughout the scriptures, LDS Church publications, and writings of the prophets. See www.lds.org.

p. 3, *The Family: A Proclamation to the World* is an official document, copyright 1995 by The Church of Jesus Christ of Latter-day Saints, which includes the note, "This proclamation was read by Gordon B. Hinckley as part of his message at the General Relief Society Meeting held September 23, 1995, in Salt Lake City, Utah."

p. 4, *For the Strength of Youth* is an official publication of The Church of Jesus Christ of Latter-day Saints, 2001. Quote is found on p. 26.

p. 6, George Orwell wrote, "All societies, as the price of survival, have to insist on a fairly high standard of sexual morality. . . . Society has always to demand a little more from human beings than it will get in practice." (*Collection of Essays,* "The Art of Donald McGill," Harcourt, New York, 1946.) Also see "Two Lists" by Janice Graham which correlates 25 differences between a sexually moral and a sexually immoral society at www.standardofliberty.org/janice45.htm.

p. 7, The Articles of Faith are found at the end of The Pearl of Great Price.

p.8, The first and great commandment to love God is also found in Deuteronomy 6:4-5, Mark 12:29-30, Luke 10:27, Luke 11:42, John 5:42-43, D&C 20:18-19, and referred to throughout the scriptures.

Chapter 2: Me Tarzan, You Jane

p. 11, For further study on God's timeless absolutes, read *The Abolition of Man* by C. S. Lewis, HarperCollins, New York, 1944. See a short review of this book by Janice Graham on www.standardofliberty.org/janice34.htm.

p. 11, The California bill that declares the words mother and father obsolete is Senate Bill777.

p. 11, The story about the little boy being allowed to present himself as a girl is reported by Julia Reischel, "See Tom Be Jane," villagevoice.com, May 30, 2006.

p. 12-13, For a great article on how language has been exploited by the sexual activist movement see "Deciphering 'Gay' Word-Speak and Language of Confusion," by Scott D. Lively at www.newswithviews.com/conspiracy/conspiracy6.htm.

p. 13, Concerning the important differences between mothers and fathers, see Dr. A. Dean Byrd, "Gender Complementarity and Child Rearing: Where Tradition and Science Agree," 2005. http://www.narth.com/docs/gendercomplementarity.html.

p. 14, References to the distinctness of male and female and their gender roles are also found in Matthew 19: 4-6 and throughout the scriptures.

p. 14, *The Family: A Proclamation to the World* is an official document, copyright 1995 by The Church of Jesus Christ of Latter-day Saints, which includes the note, "This proclamation was read by President Gordon B. Hinckley as part of his message at the General Relief Society Meeting held September 23, 1995, in Salt Lake City, Utah." See www.lds.org for many more references from the prophets about the reality of male and female.

p. 15, The report about the mummy is found at http://cryptoworld.co.uk/manchester-university-helps-dna-test-hatshepsut-mummy/.

p. 16, "And by the power of the Holy Ghost ye may know the truth of all things" (Moroni 10:5). Also, John 14:26, 2 Nephi 32:5.

Chapter 3: Mirror, Mirror on a Tree

p. 20, Dr. A. Dean Byrd points out that girls will only imitate their mothers if their fathers treat their mothers well.

p. 20, For further study on the societal and political importance of marriage and the conjugal family, read *The Natural Family, a Manifesto* by Allan Carlson and Paul Mero, The Howard Center, Rockford, Illinois, 2007, at http://familymanifesto.net/. Also see "Propaganda, Freedom, and the Heterogenous Family," by Janice Graham at www.standardofliberty.org/janice20.htm.

p. 22, Some officially organized groups based on self-identification with "alternative sexual orientations" include Human Rights Campaign; Gay, Lesbian and Straight Education Network (GLSEN); Seicus; ACT-UP; Equality Utah; Lambda Legal; National Gay and Lesbian Task Force; Gay and Lesbian Alliance Against Defamation (GLAAD), Parents, Families, and Friends of Lesbians and Gays (PFLAGG), Gay Pride.

p. 23, For further study about the importance of boys developing proper masculinity read *Men and Marriage* by George Gilder, Pelican Publishing Company, Gretna, Louisiana, 1986. Also see a three-part article, "Arming Prince Charming," by Janice Graham at www.standardofliberty.org/janice24.htm.

p. 24-25, The Articles of Faith are found at the end of The Pearl of Great Price.

p. 27, A wonderful children's book that sensitively addresses the issue of little boys and girls having interests that cross over is *Impunity Jane* by Rumer Godden,Viking Press, New York, 1954.

Chapter 4: Were You Raised in a Jungle?

p. 32, For further study on God's timeless absolutes, read *The Abolition of Man* by C. S. Lewis, HarperCollins, New York, 1944 and his *Mere Christianity,* HarperSan Francisco, 19433, Bk IV, ch.8.

p. 33, William Golding's novel, *Lord of the Flies,* was originally published in 1954. Golding won the 1983 Nobel Prize for literature mostly for this book.

p. 34, One example of a 15-year-old being given an abortion through her school without her parents' knowledge or consent can be found at Judicial Watch Blog, "Public School Helps Girl Get Abortion," www.judicialwatch.org/blog/2010/mar/public-school-helps-girl-get-abortion.

p. 34, For education on America's moral decline, read *Slouching Towards Gomorrah* by Robert H. Bork, ReganBooks, 1996.

p. 34, George Orwell wrote, "All societies, as the price of survival, have to insist on a fairly high standard of sexual morality. . . . Society has always to demand a little more from human beings than it will get in practice." (Collection of Essays, "The Art of Donald McGill," Harcourt, New York, 1946.)

Chapter 5: Loincloths, Etc.

p. 39, Joe J. Christensen, in "Greed, Selfishness, and Overindulgence," *Ensign,* May 1999, 9, talks about enjoying the fashions of the day without going to extremes. Also Gordon B. Hinckley, in "A Prophet's Counsel and a Prayer for Youth," Ensign, Jan 2001, 2.

p. 40, *For the Strength of Youth* is an official publication of The Church of Jesus Christ of Latter-day Saints, 2001. This reference is found on p. 22.

p. 40, One of many articles written about the rise of young people "sexting" is "Teens and Cell Phones," by David E. Smith, the Illinois Family Institute, 2009, at www.illnoisfamily.org/news/contentview.asp?c=34325.

p. 42, A wonderful resource for learning how to separate our great spiritual worth as children of God from external conditions and events is contained in James B. Cox's tapes and workbook, *Becoming Spiritually Centered and Overcoming the World* (1997), and his book, *How to Qualify for the Celestial Kingdom Today* (1983) available at National Marketing, Inc., www.nmiut.net.

Chapter 6: Think Before You Swing

p. 44, The characters Tarzan and Jane, originally created by author Edgar Rice Burroughs in his early 1900s novels, are in the public domain.

p. 46, The short novel, *A Separate Peace,* by John Knowles was first published in 1959.

p. 47, A famous treatise on the power to choose our thoughts and attitudes is portrayed in the book, *Man's Search for Meaning* by Viktor E. Frankl who endured years in Nazi death camps, and was first published by Simon and Schuster, New York, 1959.

Chapter 7: No Time for Monkey Business

p. 52, A wonderful resource for learning how to separate our great spiritual worth from external conditions and events is contained in James B. Cox's tapes and workbook, *Becoming Spiritually Cen-*

tered and Overcoming the World (1997), and his book, *How to Qualify for the Celestial Kingdom Today* (1983) available at National Marketing, Inc., www.nmiut.net.

p. 55, For more about LDS leaders' counsel on dating, see *For the Strength of Youth,* 24.

p. 56, See Dallin H. Oaks, "Dating Versus Hanging Out," *Ensign,* June 2006, p 10-16.

Chapter 8: Wild Elephant!

p. 63, The movie referred to is *The Hudsucker Proxy,* 1994. See an article by Janice Graham, "You Know, For Kids," at www.standardofliberty.org/janice32.htm.

p. 63, Some of the dangerous and inappropriate materials about sex and sexuality distributed to elementary school age kids are:

Robie H. Harris, *It's Perfectly Normal,* Candlewick Press, Cambridge, MA, 1996.

Leslie Newman, *Heather Has Two Mommies,* Alyson Publications, 2000.

Linda DeHaan, *King and King,* Tricycle Press, 2002.

Michael Willhoite, *Daddy's Roommate,* Btbound, 1991.

It's Elementary: Talking About Gay Issues in School, a training video for teachers endorsed by the National Education Association, made in 1997.

p. 63, To learn about the results of sex education in schools read Barbara Dafoe Whitehead's excellent article, "The Failure of Sex

Education," *Atlantic Monthly,* Oct 1994, www.theatlantic.com/past/politics/family/failure.htm.

p. 66, The information from the Center for Disease Control can be found at http://www.cdc.gov/mmwr/preview/mmwrhtml/ss5609a1.htm.

p. 66, Gordon B. Hinckley said, "Pornography, with its sleazy filth, sweeps over the earth like a horrible, engulfing tide" (Gordon B. Hinckley, "Some Thoughts on Temples, Retention of Converts, and Missionary Service," Ensign, Nov 1997, 49).

p. 67, For more understanding about the dangerous spread of pornography, read *A War We Must Win,* by John Harmer, Bookcraft, Salt Lake City, 1999.

p. 69, Dr. Victor Cline has prepared a pamphlet called, "Pornography's Effects on Adults and Children" which can be found at http://obscenitycrimes.org/cline_unabridged.pdf.

p.69, Dr. Matthew Hedelius was quoted in an article by Anna Cheng-Yen, "Broken Families," The Herald Journal, Feb 20,2006.

p. 70, This quote is from the movie, *Indiana Jones and the Raiders of the Lost Ark,* 1981.

p. 73, Spencer W. Kimball writes about masturbation in *The Miracle of Forgiveness,* Bookcraft, Salt Lake City, 77-78.

p. 75, Additional scriptures condemning homosexual behaviors: Genesis 19:4-9, Judges 19:22-24, Leviticus 20:13, Deuteronomy 23:17-18.

p. 75, For statements condemning homosexuality in thought, desire, and deed from LDS Church presidencies and apostles, see www.lds.org and search homosexuality. There are almost 300 references listed. For starters, may we suggest: Spencer W. Kimball, "President Kimball Speaks Out on Morality," *The New Era,* Nov 1980, 39; James E. Faust, "Serving the Lord and Resisting the Devil," *Ensign,* Sep 1995, 2; Boyd K. Packer, "Ye Are the Temple of God," *Ensign,* Nov 2000, 72-74. More recently, see the 2007 (copyright 2006) Relief Society/Priesthood Manual, *Teachings of the Presidents of the Church: Spencer W. Kimball,* Chapter 17: "The Law of Chastity," 178. See also *For the Strength of Youth,* 28. A succinct compilation is found in *Homosexuality and the Church of Jesus Christ,* by Dr. A. Dean Byrd, Cedar Fort, 2001.

p. 76, See "The First Presidency Statement on Same-Gender Marriage," *Ensign,* March, 2004.

p. 76, To understand the gay agenda see "Overhauling Straight America," Nov 1987, by gay activists Kirk and Pill, www.article8.org/docs/gay_strategies/overhauling.htm or the book, *After the Ball* by gay activists Kirk and Madsen, Penguin, 1989. Also, *The Homosexual Agenda, Exposing the Principal Threat to Religious Freedom Today,* by Alan Sears and Craig Osten, Broadman and Holman, Nashville, 2003. See also, "Somewhere over the Rainbow—that's where you'll find the truth about 'gayness'" by Janice Graham at www.standardofliberty.org/janice21.htm and "The New Homosexuality: A Fabrication with a Diabolical End" at www.standardofliberty.org/janice33.htm.

p. 76, Concerning claims that nonacceptance of homosexuality causes suicide, see G. Remafidi, J. A. Farrow, R.W. Deisher, "Risk Factors for Attempted Suicide in Gay and Bisexual Youth," *Pediatrics 87,* 1991, 869-875. It reports that for each year a young person puts off the gay label, his risk of suicide decreases 20%.

p. 77, To find a list of diseases related to homosexual behavior see www.glma.org and click on "Top Ten Issues to Discuss with Your Health Care Provider."

p. 77, A report about shortened life expectancy among men who engage in homosexual sex is from *The Oxford University International Journal of Epidemiology* "ije.oxfordjournals.org, "Modeling the impact of HIV disease on mortality in gay and bisexual men," 1997.

p. 77, On Feb. 8, 2008 Matt Foremen, head of the National Gay and Lesbian Task Force, at a NGLTF conference stated, "Folks, with 70% of the people in this country living with HIV being gay or bi, we cannot deny that HIV is a gay disease. We have to own that and face up to that." In 2006 Lorri Jean, CEO of the Gay and Lesbian Center in Los Angeles said, "HIV is a gay disease. Own it. End it." See Concerned Women for America. www.cwfa.org and wwwctv.ca.

p. 78, This quote is from Letter from The First Presidency, "Standards of Morality and Fidelity," Salt Lake City: The Church of Jesus Christ of Latter-day Saints, Nov 1991.

p. 79, The high rate of success in overcoming homosexual tendencies is chronicled in *Ex-Gays? An Extended Longitudinal Study of Attempted Religiously Mediated Change in Sexual Orientation,* Jones and Yarhouse, 2007.

p. 79, Dr. Neil L. Whitehead prepared an excellent scholarly presentation called *Born That Way?* in 2007 which can be viewed at www.standardofliberty.org. Download his book, *My Genes Made Me Do It!* at www.mygenes.co.nz which shows that homosexuality cannot be biologically innate or fixed. See also, A. Dean Byrd, Shirley E. Cox, Jeffrey W. Robinson, "Homosexuality: The Innate-Immutability Argument Finds No Basis in Science," Salt Lake Tribune, May 27, 2001, found at www.narth.com/docs/innate.html.

Chapter 9: Savage or Saint?

p. 81, These quotes are from *Mere Christianity* by C. S. Lewis, HarperSan Francisco, 1943, p. 198.

p. 83, Eminent LDS scholar High Nibley, talks about human imperfection in the documentary, *The Faith of an Observer, Conversations with Hugh Nibley,* Covenant Communications, 2004.

p. 86, Read about Anti-Christs in The Book of Mormon in Jacob 7 (Sherem), Alma 1 (Nehor), and Alma 30 (Korihor).

p. 87-8, The Articles of Faith are found at the end of The Pearl of Great Price.

p. 89, Concerning human attempts to utopianize the world, Monsignor Gilbey said,"The duty of the Christian is not to leave the world a better place but to leave the world a better man." Quoted by Roger Scruton in *Gentle Regrets,* Continuum, New York, 2006.

p. 91, "The Prayer of Cyrus Brown" was written by Sam Walter Foss (1858-1911). Thanks, Dad.

p. 92, Scriptures about praying always: Luke 18:1, Luke 21:36, 2 Nephi 32:9, 3 Nephi 18:15, 18-21, Alma 34:27, D&C 19:38, D&C 93:49.

p. 94, More effective prayer is explained in James B. Cox's workbook, *Becoming Spiritually Centered and Overcoming the World* (1997) available at National Marketing, Inc., www.nmiut.net.

p. 95, For an excellent description of the work of the Holy Ghost, see *Key to the Science of Theology,* by Parley P. Pratt, p. 100. Also see the August 1978 *Ensign,*"I Have a Question," p.32-3 by Don Norton for two good lists, one of positive results of having the Spirit and the other of negative effects of not having the Spirit. You might want to post this list where the family can see it often.

p. 96, The sacrament prayers are found in Doctrine & Covenants 20:77, 79.

p. 96, The first and great commandment to love God is also found in Deuteronomy 6:4-5, Matthew 22: 37-8, Luke 10:27, Luke 11:42, John 5:42-43, D&C 20:18-19, and referred to throughout the scriptures.

p. 100, For a statement from Gordon B. Hinckley on the responsibility to serve a mission see, Gordon B. Hinckley, "Some Thoughts on Temples, Retention of Converts, and Missionary Service," *Ensign,* Nov 1997, 49.

p. 102, See *The Miracle of Forgiveness,* Bookcraft, Salt Lake City, 1969 by Spencer W. Kimball for information about sexual sin in regards to serving a mission.

p. 104, A striking illustration of intense nonsexual love between two men occurs in the 1960 movie, *Spartacus,* in the moving scene when Spartacus and Antoninus are captured by Roman soldiers.

Chapter 11: A Treehouse of Your Own

p. 106, President Joseph F. Smith said, "Teach that the law of chastity is one of the most vital importance, both to children, and to men and to women. It is a vitally important principle to the children of God in all their lives, from the cradle to the grave (Joseph F. Smith, *Gospel Doctrine,* 1939, 273).

p. 108, For further study on the societal and political importance of marriage and the conjugal family, read *The Natural Family, a Manifesto* by Allan Carlson and Paul Mero, The Howard Center, Rockford, Illinois, 2007, at http://familymanifesto.net/. Also see "Propaganda, Freedom, and the Heterogenous Family," by Janice Graham at www.standardofliberty.org/janice20.htm.

p. 110, See "First Presidency Statement on Same-Gender Marriage," 2004, at http://newsroom.lds.org/ldsnewroom/eng/news-releases-stories/first-presidency-statement-on-same-gender-marriage.

p. 110, David A. Bednar said "The natures of male and female spirits complete and perfect each other, and therefore, men and women are intended to progress together toward exhaltation.""Marriage is Essential to His Eternal Plan," *Ensign,* June 2006, 82.

p. 112, The quote from Gordon B. Hinckley is from "Look to the Future," *Ensign,* Nov.1997, 67.

Chapter 12: The One Right Path

p. 117, *America's Godly Heritage* is an excellent family video prepared by David Barton. It can be found at www.wallbuilders.com. Also see his book, *Original Intent: The Courts, the Constitution, and Religion,* Wallbuilder Press, 2008.

p. 118, There are many good books about how America's schools and universities have become infiltrated with revisionist history, anti-traditional values, anti-American, and anti-God indoctrination, including sexual liberation, and how education systems are abusing their own academic freedom policies. May we suggest *America's Schools, The Battleground for Freedom* by Allen Quist, Edwatch, 2005, and *One-Party Classroom, How Radical Professors at America's Top Colleges Indoctrinate Students and Undermine Our Democracy,* by David Horowitz and Jacob Laksin, Random House, 2009.

p. 118, See "The Wares of Knowledge: Traditional Versus Transformational Education" by Janice Graham at www.standardofliberty.org/janice38.htm.

p. 121, For information on science's progress since Darwin's theory of evolution, see *Darwin's Black Box* by Michael J. Behe, Free Press, 2006. Also see *Darwin's Dilemma* and *Unlocking the Mystery of Life,* documentaries found at www.illustramedia.com/ddinfo.htm and www.illustramedia.com/umolinfo.htm.

p. 122, *The Privileged Planet* is an inspiring 60-minute documentary about Earth's uniquely favored position in the universe, testifying through science of God as Creator. Find it at www.illustramedia.com/tppinfo.htm.

p. 123, The quote from Brigham Young is found in *Journal of Discourses,* Vol 12, 34.

p. 124, The reference to C. S. Lewis is from his book, *That Hideous Strength,* Macmillan Publishing Co., Inc., New York, 1946, 72.

p. 125, See *Anne Frank: The Diary of a Young Girl,* Doubleday, New York, 1993, 256.

Janice Barrett Graham is a mother of seven and grandmother of 15. She is married to Stephen Franklin Graham, a CPA and president of the Standard of Liberty Foundation. This is her fifth book. An award-winning writer, she has had dozens of articles and stories appear in regional and national publications including the top children's magazines such as the Cricket Group, *Highlights for Children,* and also *The Friend.* See more of her writing at www.standardofliberty.org.